Better Together gave me much-needed confidence to create a community of moms to do life with. We were not meant to do life alone!

CHRISTINA EASTMAN, *husband-supporter, ever-present mama, wannabe sitcom writer*

As a frequent mover, it's often difficult to start over, building new relationships grassroots-style. *Better Together* offered great tips on how to proactively create community rather than waiting for new community to find me. A great reminder to prioritize sisterhood, because we are, indeed, better together than we are alone.

BRENDA OTTINGER, *loving wife, grateful mom of noise and dirt (read: boys), fledgling blogger, cupcake lover*

Jill is a wonderful, close friend to me. She is genuine to the core and lives what she writes about friendship. I believe we should always have friends of all ages, and I joke that we especially need to have younger friends so we have someone to visit us in the nursing home! *Better Together* teaches you how to be that kind of friend and have that kind of friends!

BECKY GLENN, *collector of friends, older than most of you reading this, thankful to do life with God, has been known to wear a conehead on occasion!*

Better Together is a very practical, candid, honest book about why it's important to have your "mom tribe." Anne and Jill do a great job speaking on how to develop the friendships we all crave in the society we live in today. Even though I'm a grandma now, it reminded me that we should not mother (or grandmother) alone! Friendships enrich our lives and challenge us to become better women overall.

BONNIE MILLER, *mom of two, grandma of one, and enjoying being an empty nester!*

Jill's newest book for moms encouraged me to think about the importance of relationships with other moms. *Better Together* showed me that it does not matter if you are an Innie or an Outie (you'll see), we all have our stuff somewhere! We all need mom community no matter the stage of mothering!

KARLA P., *wife, mom, family childcare provider*

Better Together reminded me of all the great times we had together as moms raising kids, and I thank the Lord I had such good friends to help me along. Jill is the best mentor I could ever have hoped for. I'm a better mom because of her guidance, and she's still helping me as a grandparent!

BETH H., *wife, mom, grandma, child of God, and the Purple Cat Lady*

better together

Because You're Not Meant to Mom Alone

JILL SAVAGE

with ANNE McCLANE

MOODY PUBLISHERS

CHICAGO

Published in association with the literary agency of Transatlantic Agency.

Edited by Elizabeth Cody Newenhuyse
Interior and cover design: Erik M. Peterson
Cover: photo by Tami Paige / lettering by Connie Gabbert
Photo of Jill Savage and Anne McClaine by Tami Paige

Library of Congress Cataloging-in-Publication Data
Savage, Jill, 1964- author.
Better together : because you're not meant to mom alone / by Jill Savage ; with Anne (Savage) McClane.
  pages cm
Includes bibliographical references.
ISBN 978-0-8024-1379-6
1. Motherhood—Religious aspects—Christianity. 2. Female friendship—Religious aspects—Christianity. 3. Parenting—Religious aspects—Christianity. I. Title.
BV4529.18.S237 2016
248.8'431—dc23
                      2015033764

We hope you enjoy this book from Moody Publishers. Our goal is to provide high-quality, thought-provoking books and products that connect truth to your real needs and challenges. For more information on other books and products written and produced from a biblical perspective, go to www.moodypublishers.com or write to:

Moody Publishers
820 N. LaSalle Boulevard
Chicago, IL 60610

1 3 5 7 9 10 8 6 4 2

Printed in the United States of America

THIS BOOK IS DEDICATED TO

ALL OF THE WOMEN WHO HAVE BEEN

A PART OF OUR MOTHERING COMMUNITIES.

WE'RE BOTH BETTER MOMS BECAUSE WE

DID LIFE TOGETHER WITH EACH OF YOU.

CONTENTS

## CHAPTER 1

Where It All Begins

O ne year after our first Hearts at Home conference, I found myself driving across town alone in my filthy minivan filled with car seats and five weeks' worth of Sunday school papers. I was having a conversation with God about the unexpected place He had me. I was leading a moms group in our church that had held what was supposed to be, a one time conference for moms. We expected 400 moms to attend and 1,100 showed up. It seemed that God's vision was much bigger than mine. We were now within a few weeks of our second conference and over 2,800 women had already registered to attend! We had assembled a board of directors, incorporated as a nonprofit, and were growing faster than I felt I could keep up with.

"You have to be laughing, God," I exclaimed with a mix of humor and resignation. "You now have me leading a huge ministry to moms and I DON'T EVEN LIKE WOMEN!"

I'm a late bloomer when it comes to female relationships. Growing up, most of the kids in our neighborhood were boys. My two sisters and I played softball with the neighborhood guys in the empty lot next to our house nearly every night during the spring, summer, and fall. Even though I went to all twelve years of school in the same school district, I never had one girlfriend who was my "best friend since first grade" as some people have.

I did have friends who were girls. I went to a few birthday parties and sleepovers over the years. Some girls eventually moved into the neighborhood and we had fun together . . . playing baseball in the side lot. I also had some girlfriends I ate lunch with in high school.

Maybe it was growing up in a neighborhood of boys, or maybe it was being attracted to the simplicity of guy friendships, but female friendships weren't exactly a priority for me. I liked my guy friendships because they seemed to be less complicated. These weren't boyfriends . . . just guy friends who didn't get their feelings hurt easily, communicated at face value, and protected me fiercely. They were more like the big brothers I never had.

What do I do when I feel left out even as an adult?

I met some friends late in high school and I spent a year living in a sorority my freshman year of college (that, honestly, never really met my friendship expectations), but I never seemed to really "click" with the whole girlfriend thing in my younger years. While I privately longed to have girlfriends to share secrets with, laugh together, and talk on the phone for hours, I summed it up in my mind that I just wasn't meant to have many girlfriends and I needed to be content with what I had.

And then I became a mom.

Suddenly I had this desire to spend time with other women who understood what my life is like. I needed to learn from them. I needed to know if what my kid was doing was normal. I needed to know if my feelings were okay. More than anything, I needed to know I wasn't alone! Seeking female friendships to meet those needs, I discovered that I longed for a mothering community around me, but I had no idea how to find one.

I stumbled my way through those early years of mom friendships. I lived far from family, so my friends became family. I experienced both the high of "doing life" with other moms and the low of being rejected by some I thought were my friends. I've made lifelong friends and experienced friendship "breakups." I've come to learn that my personality and temperament affect the number of friends I will likely have. I've discovered that some friendships are seasonal and others are lifelong. Finally, I've learned some strategies along the way for making friends, keeping friends, and even understanding when it's okay to let a friendship go. I hope you're ready to dig into all of that, because the truth is, we need each other. We need to be with other women who understand our world of mothering, but most of us struggle with some aspect of making those relationships work.

Friendships change as motherhood changes. That's why I'm glad to have my daughter Anne writing with me. Anne just turned thirty. She's been married nine years and is the mother of a preschooler and a kindergartner. Anne has moved to a new community in the past eighteen months and has been knee-deep in forging new friendships. She's also never known motherhood without social media and the reality of "friend" being both a noun and a verb. Anne is an at-home mom who runs a day care in her home. Her experiences and season of life will likely resonate with some of you.

I, on the other hand, am just on the edge of the empty-nest season of life. With my youngest in college, I'm discovering a new season of life where friendships are no longer knit together by our kids' activities. Many women in my season of life are working full-time, which greatly factors into this friendship thing as well.

Anne and I have collaborated throughout the book, but we've chosen to write only in my voice. Anne's stories are woven in and out of chapters, but some of Anne's are also set off by themselves in ways that will help present a concept you can think about more deeply. We hope this makes reading easier for you!

Anne and I asked our online communities what challenges they found in mom friendships and what topics they would like to see addressed on these pages. I bet you can relate to some of these:

- How can we pursue relational depth without the drama?
- What do I do when I feel left out even as an adult?
- How do I find time to build friendships?
- How do I take a friendship deeper?
- What do we do with the comparing we tend to do in friendships?

These are great questions and we're going to dig into every one of them plus more! Most of us face relational struggles in some way. Too often we think we're the only ones struggling, but that's not true at all. We're just not exactly willing to advertise, "Hey, I'm struggling with friendships" on Facebook, in our Bible study, or even in our moms group for fear of appearing like we don't have it together.

Looking back over the past thirty years of mothering five children, I can truly say I am who I am because of the women who have been in my life. I'm glad I pushed through the struggles, chose to risk again after being hurt, and learned some relational wisdom to navigate the sometimes-rocky waters. My mom friends have grown me in my organizational skills, my parenting, my marriage, and my spiritual life. I've been cared for, encouraged, corrected, and loved on by the women in my life. More than anything else, I've truly come to understand that we really are better together.

WHY ARE MOM FRIENDS SO IMPORTANT?

There's a new business in the community I live in that gathers women together to make freezer meals in a home party type of setting. I'm not a home party girl at all, but when I'm going to end up with ten meals in the freezer in less than ninety minutes and someone else does the shopping, food prep, and cleanup, you've got my attention! I put an event invitation out on Facebook and had twenty women join me at a party I hosted. Most of the ladies who came didn't know one another because they were all from different parts of my life—some from church, some from a moms group I used to go to, some from Hearts at Home where I work, some from online relationships I've built, and a few women came because they were friends of someone who was coming.

As we assembled the main dishes for these meals, we broke down into five groups of four. Each group was in charge of assembling two of the recipes. We formed an assembly line of sorts, putting together twenty of each recipe. After the first five minutes, you would have never known that these ladies didn't know each other. The buzz of conversation was electric. There was laughter, stories, and wisdom being shared. Toward the end of the party someone said, "This is so much fun! I'm sure this is what it used to be like when women would cook together more often."

A century ago, extended family often formed a woman's natural mothering community. While quilting with aunts and sisters-in-law, marriage wisdom was passed along. While cooking with your mom and grandmother, parenting knowledge was shared. While scrubbing clothes with sisters and friends, homemaking tips were discussed. If a mom was sick, her community helped care for her kids. When a new baby was born, the village fed and cared for the new mom and her family. When there was a big project to accomplish, her tribe of mothers pulled together to help.

Today, many of us live away from our moms, aunts, sisters, and in-laws. Families are more independent in carrying out their household responsibilities. Even if a mom lives near her family, many older women are now in the workforce and just don't have the time or the opportunity to be together in the day to day—which is what it takes for regular interaction and natural conversation to happen.

Because our mothering community is no longer formed naturally within extended family relationships, we have to pursue, discover, and assemble it ourselves. We have to recognize the value of it and make it a priority in our lives because we're stronger, wiser, and even healthier when we have a mom community around us.

THE BENEFITS OF FRIENDSHIP

It was Eleanor Roosevelt who said, "Many people will walk in and out of your life; but only true friends will leave footprints in your heart." Those footprints represent the impact, the influence, and the inspiration our friends give us. Exactly how are our lives enriched by friendship? Here are ten powerful benefits of friendship:

Benefit #1: Connection

Many women tell us that when they attended a Hearts at Home mom conference for the first time, they found themselves crying within the first few minutes of the conference. There's truly nothing happening that is that tear-producing, and many report that they are not really criers at all, but the impact of being with thousands of other moms and suddenly realizing you're really not alone is almost more than the heart can handle. The emotional response overflows in tears.

> *When you give to a friendship, it's usually because you want to.*

Being with like-minded people who really do understand your life in some way is very powerful. Having someone to talk with and share interests with adds so much richness to your life. Friendships keep us connected to the world outside of our home and family. They help us remember the important things in life and provide much-needed perspective no matter how we choose to connect.

Benefit #2: A Sense of Belonging

The human soul longs to belong. We want to know that people believe in us, approve of us, and accept us for who we are. Friendships provide a place where we're needed, we're contributing, and we're really known.

They also allow us to be a part of something bigger than ourselves. We can align with others who have the same beliefs, experiences, and interests. Sometimes we band with others to accomplish something together that we couldn't accomplish on our own. The "team spirit" we experience contributes to our sense of belonging. "We did this together!" might be said internally or aloud.

However, belonging doesn't just come from being a part of a group. It can be felt in smaller circles of friends as well. Small gestures, like when a friend sends you a text that she's thinking of you, communicate you're important to someone, being thought of, and are a part of their world.

Benefit #3: The Ability to Give

When you care about and care for other people, it brings a sense of satisfaction to your own life. Your contribution to another person's well-being, your encouraging words, your physical help all contribute to your feeling of being needed.

We all need relationships we can contribute to. Yes, as a mom you're giving all the time, but that kind of giving is somewhat "required." When you give to a friendship, it's usually because you want to.

When we give to others, we feel closer to them. That "interconnectedness" builds a sense of community in our life. Giving time, energy, and encouragement enriches our lives and increases our capacity to love.

Benefit #4: The Ability to Receive

Most of us are much more comfortable giving than receiving. Yet, if we refuse to receive, we rob others of the joy of giving. A healthy friendship is a dance between the two.

We might receive comfort, encouragement, wisdom, knowledge, a shoulder to cry on, or practical help from a friend. Seasons of crisis may be times of receiving more than usual.

Friendships provide opportunities for us to admit our need for help. They give us the opportunity to open up our hands and our heart and allow others in. We benefit from learning to both give and receive!

Benefit #5: Sounding Board

A good friend is the perfect person to run ideas past. She can listen, share in your excitement, or bring some much-needed perspective. Sometimes we need the wisdom of others or the viewpoint of someone who isn't as close to a situation as we are to help us keep our head on straight.

Friends are the ones with whom we can also share our dreams, frustrations, and fears. They provide a safety zone where we don't have to worry about being judged. With honesty in place, a good friend can also provide much-needed accountability. Sometimes we need a swift kick in the seat of our pants if we're off track in our thinking or need to look at something from another angle.

Benefit #6: Wisdom and Experiences of Others

My friend Tonya, who has a special education degree, shared with me wisdom about learning challenges our adopted son was facing as he learned a new language at the age of nine. My friend Lora helped me sponge-paint my hallway after she perfected her technique on her living room walls. My friend Julie, who is a doula, prepared me to be Anne's birth coach along with her husband, Matt. My friend Becky is a natural organizer who shares her wisdom when I'm overwhelmed and need help with a home reorganization project.

On the day I received my breast cancer diagnosis, I was an emotional mess. I ended up on my friend Crystal's doorstep. Crystal, a former nurse -

practitioner-turned-homeschooling-mom, and I have been friends for many years. I needed Crystal's comfort as a friend and her wisdom and medical knowledge as an NP. I sat at her kitchen table, called my doctor's office back, and asked them to give Crystal all the info on my biopsy. She knew and understood the medical terms and she knew the questions to ask.

Friendships fill your gaps. They allow you to tap into the strengths of others. They broaden your knowledge in so many ways.

Benefit #7: Marital Health

Husbands make terrible girlfriends, and honestly it's unfair to expect them to be something they're not meant to be. Women and men communicate differently. If he's like the majority of men, your husband will likely communicate factually. He'll want to fix any problems you talk to him about. He's great at giving you three ways to proceed.

A girlfriend, however, will likely communicate emotionally. She'll listen and empathize with your challenges. She'll make sure you know you're not alone as you journey through motherhood.

Not only that, but there are activities that your husband may not enjoy as much as you do, that a girlfriend might enjoy doing with you. If your husband isn't into going to the theatre, picking strawberries, or garage sale-ing, it might be better to do those things with a girlfriend who enjoys them as much as you do!

Benefit #8: Spiritual Health

A good friend can encourage you to keep your eyes on God's truth when you're tempted to believe the lies of the enemy. She can pray with and for you. She can send a Bible verse just when you need it.

The Bible tells us "Two are better than one, because they have a good return for their labor. If either of them falls down, one can help the other up" (Ecclesiastes 4:9–10a NIV). When faith is part of a friendship, you're able to share what God is teaching you and spur each other on to grow deeper spiritually. This benefit shores up the foundation of our life. Even if the friendship fades, the spiritual benefit can last a lifetime.

Benefit #9: Emotional Health

Knowing someone cares makes such a difference in how we feel about ourselves. Friendship increases self-esteem, and good friends can even help you break a pattern of destructive self-talk, if you struggle with that. While it's entirely possible and even probable that you'll sometimes feel lonely even when you have friends, friendship staves off the general feeling of loneliness that can often contribute to depression and anxiety.

I didn't know her at ALL, but knew of her. She'd recently delivered a stillborn baby. One Sunday a video was shown in church promoting small groups. In the video, a woman who'd had a stillborn baby shared her story. My chest tightened watching the video and knowing the mom who had recently delivered a stillborn baby was in the room. I saw her get up and walk out of the room. I knew I couldn't let her just be alone. I met her in the bathroom and just hugged her. (And I was not a "huggy" person back then!) One year later, I buried my own child after a household accident. She was the one who met me at church the next Sunday. I even remember the sweater she was wearing. It's been fourteen years since that first hug in the bathroom and she's still one of my best friends.
—CHRISTY

Friends can help create emotional stability. When you weather the ups and downs of life with someone who cares, you feel stronger than if you were navigating life on your own. Just knowing you have someone in your corner can help you feel more capable and confident in handling the challenges you face.

Benefit #10: Physical Health

It's no secret that friends are good for your emotional health, but did you know they are also good for your physical health? Though both men and women respond to stress physically with the fight-or-flight response, women also respond by producing brain chemicals that cause them to seek out friendships with other women, a UCLA study[1] suggests. The study discovered that when the hormone oxytocin is released as part of the stress response in a woman, it encourages her to tend children and gather with women. And when she "tends and befriends," more oxytocin is released, which actually calms her and reduces stress.[2]

Other studies have found that social ties reduce our risk of disease by lowering blood pressure, heart rate, and cholesterol. In one study, for example, researchers found that people who had no friends increased their risk of death. So hanging out with friends can actually help us live longer![3]

It also appears that friends help us live better. The Harvard Medical School Nurses' Health Study found that the more friends a woman had, the less likely she was to develop physical challenges as she got older. In fact, the results were so significant, the researchers determined that not having close friends or confidants was as damaging to your health as smoking or carrying extra weight.

You and I will not have a single friend who will bring all of these benefits to our lives. We'll likely not experience these all at once either. However, over time and with a commitment to investing in friendships, we'll experience many of them in our lifetime!

YOU'RE NOT ALONE

Our youngest son was home from college for the summer. He had just celebrated his one-year "anniversary" of dating his girlfriend. As he was helping me cut up vegetables for dinner, I asked, "So, Austin, what are you planning on reading this summer?" "Reading?" he responded with indignation. "I'm taking an online class and that's all the reading I'm doing this summer." The next week he declared that the girlfriend signed them both up for the adult summer reading program at the local library and he thought it was a great idea. We've had dozens of other "crazy mom/smart girlfriend" interactions over the past few months. In exasperation, I told him I was going to write a blog post about the fact that everything I suggest to him he thinks is a ridiculous idea, and everything his girlfriend suggests he thinks is a great idea. He said, "Mom, what would the purpose of a blog post like that even be?" "To let other moms know they're not alone," I responded, determining to get that post written sooner rather than later.

You. Are. Not. Alone. Those four words are powerful for moms. We wonder if our kids are normal. We wonder if other moms feel like we sometimes feel. We wonder if our marriage is the only marriage having issues. We long to know that we're not the only mom who's driven somewhere and realized the car seat wasn't buckled in, or has forgotten her kid at school, or has fed her family cereal for dinner. We all need the reassurance that happens when "momming together" as we share real-life stuff, and realize we aren't alone.

Recently I had lunch with a dear friend. We both have kids who struggle with mental health issues. I was almost fearful to meet her at a restaurant because I'd been on the verge of tears for several days after a trying week with our child. I didn't want to make a fool of myself in public. Yet I knew that I needed to go. My heart needed to connect with a heart who truly understood what I was feeling. Our conversation was raw, honest, and yes some tears were shed. The remainder of the day, however, I was strong, steady, and tears weren't even close to the surface. Being reminded I wasn't alone strengthened and encouraged me in a powerful way.

Jesus taught, corrected, comforted, and served His friends.

As much as we desperately need to know we're not alone, too many of us are momming alone (and yes, I've just turned the word mom into a verb) and we don't need to be. Not only that, but we weren't created to do life alone. God created us to be in relationship with others. Jesus modeled living in community and the value of friendship. The Bible has all kinds of wisdom about friendship. We need to understand how friendship and faith go together and how to find, build, contribute to, and embrace our mothering community!

FAITH AND FRIENDSHIP

One of the most beautiful stories of friendship in the Bible is the friendship of David and Jonathan. Jonathan's father, Saul, was the first king of

Israel. Although Jonathan would have been in line to be the next king of Israel, his father's disobedience to God resulted in having the kingdom taken away from him. God chose David to be the next king of Israel. Enraged, Saul became incredibly jealous of David and set out to kill him.

Even though Jonathan knew David would be the next king, he built a friendship with him. Jonathan trusted God's decision for David to be king even if doing so resulted in his own loss of the throne. Jonathan knew of his father's hatred and intent to murder. He was such a loyal friend to David that he alerted him of the danger and saved his life (you can read the whole story in 1 Samuel 18–23). Jonathan's loyalty was an incredible gift to David. He risked his own life to protect David's life, causing Saul to eventually turn his anger toward his own son. Jonathan and David had to eventually part ways out of necessity. Their story is one of loyalty, courage, and sacrifice.

Another beautiful story of friendship is the story of Ruth and Naomi. Ruth was married to Naomi's son. Ruth and Naomi both became widows when both of their husbands died. When Naomi decided to return to her home country of Israel, Ruth insisted on going with her. Even though Ruth was not an Israelite, she accepted the God of Israel as her God and the Israelite people as her people. She did not want to lose her friend Naomi, so the two women returned to Israel together grieving, deeply for their mutual loss.

Although Naomi initially resisted Ruth's loyalty and encouraged her to return to her own people, she eventually grew to appreciate her daughter-in-law's tenacity and commitment. Eventually one of Naomi's relatives, Boaz, fell in love with Ruth. Their marriage brought incredible joy to both women.

However, it is the story of Jesus that gives us the most beautiful picture of doing life together. At the age of thirty, Jesus began His three years of public ministry before His death on the cross for us. Jesus was not a lone ranger. He did life with His disciples as well as other friends like Mary, Martha, and Lazarus.

Jesus' relationship with the disciples was both a teacher-student relationship and a friendship. Jesus called the Twelve that He "did life with" His friends. They traveled together, shared meals, and attended weddings. Jesus taught, corrected, comforted, and served His friends.

Jesus also experienced the hard side of friendship. He cried when He heard that His friend Lazarus had died. He was betrayed by His friend Judas. Peter rejected Him when he denied being Jesus' friend. His friends let Him down when they promised to pray with Him in the garden of Gethsemane but fell asleep instead.

So Jesus understands the reality of what it's like to live with people—the good and the hard. One of my favorite verses that drives this home is Hebrews 4:14–16, and I particularly love the way it is worded in *The Message*: "Now that we know what we have—Jesus, this great High Priest with ready access to God—let's not let it slip through our fingers. We don't have a priest who is out of touch with our reality. He's been through weakness and testing, experienced it all—all but the sin. So let's walk right up to him and get what he is so ready to give. Take the mercy, accept the help."

Jesus modeled living in community and the value of friendship. He dealt with the realities of living life with imperfect people. You and I need to know how to find, build, and use our mothering community to the fullest. Turn the page and let's dig into the practical side of making that happen.

FROM ANNE'S HEART

Moving into a new community where I knew no one was daunting. Through our church, we started hosting a small group for young families. (It was the one time of the week my house was actually tidied up!) We weren't sure how this group would gel: We all come from unique backgrounds and have different personalities. However, I now see how God connected the dots for us to share life together with people who are going through similar joys and challenges. We need each other and really are better together!

As a teenager, I was having a conversation with my dad about how a friend of mine only ever asked me to go shopping. We never talked about deeper stuff and never did anything outside of going to the mall together. I questioned whether this friendship was worth my time. Dad responded, "There isn't one single friend who can fill all of the friendship needs you have."

I now better understand Dad's wisdom. There will be lots of different friends filling different needs. The shopping friend. The coffeehouse-chat friend. The friend you call when your two-year-old smears poop all over her face. Some friends can fill several different needs, but none can be everything you need in a friend. That isn't fair to ask of them and it isn't possible to fulfill.

*Are you expecting one friend to fill
all your friendship needs?*

Today's Friendship Assignment

It's been said that we are to work as if everything
depends on us and pray as if everything depends
upon God. No doubt you'll be working to form,
expand, or invest in your friendships as you read
this book. When was the last time you talked to
God about your friendships?

Take just a few minutes here to thank Him for the
friends you have or pour out your heart to Him
about the friends you don't have.

He knows, He cares, and He understands.

## CHAPTER 2

Who Are You "Momming" With?

Itook six-week-old Erica to the doctor. She had been sick for a couple of days and I didn't like the sound of her cough. Anne, almost six, and Evan, almost four, accompanied me to the doctor appointment. The pediatrician examined Erica and said, "You need to go directly to the hospital. I believe she has RSV and is in respiratory distress. I will call ahead to alert them you are coming." Wow—I knew she was sick but I certainly didn't realize it was that bad! Talk about a game changer.

I called Mark at work and I called my friend Bonnie. Mark headed to the hospital to get Anne and Evan and take them to Bonnie's house. Because I was nursing Erica, I stayed with her around the clock over the next four days and that meant I missed Anne's sixth birthday. However, Bonnie filled the gap! She made a birthday cake and had a little party for Anne on her birthday while Mark and I were at the hospital with Erica. What a gift Bonnie gave to Anne—and to me! I was grateful that Bonnie and I chose to mom together.

I met Bonnie at Mom to Mom, a moms group I started eighteen months before Erica's hospital stay. Her two daughters were the same age as Anne and Evan. We traded sitting, enjoyed letting the kids play together, and always seemed to have plenty to talk about. Our friendship has lasted all these years and now we're both "grandmomming" together.

When I think of my mom community when the kids were growing up, I met my friends in many different ways. My friend Julia and I met at story hour at the library. Mindy and I met at a church event. I met Sue through my friend Janice. Marianne and I met at the park. Patti and Rita were my neighbors. Each one of these women, and others like them, formed my mom community that kept me sane, strong, and secure during the crazy years of raising kids. Some of them I'm still "momming" with, and some were in my life for a season.

There are times when looking for mom friends can feel like you're back in junior high dealing with cliques, feeling awkward, and trying to start up small-talk conversations. Too often you're attempting to do this on four hours of sleep (either because you were up with a baby or waiting for a teenager who is past curfew). Maybe you're feeling a little unqualified to be anyone's friend because you've got spit up on your shirt or you're dealing with an issue with an older kid that is causing you to feel inept at parenting. On top of that, you might be carrying all your "friendship" baggage from middle school relationships gone bad, or maybe you're like me and you just didn't have much experience with girlfriends before you became a mom. No matter what you're feeling, you need to know you're not the only one who sometimes feels the whole world has this figured out and you're the only one struggling with it.

Friendship is a progression of time, energy, and trust and only a few will make it all the way to carry a BFF label. BFFs don't drop out of the air. They start as MBFs, then move to TBFs, and then GGFs before they ever become BFFs. We need all of those kinds of friends and all levels of friendships in our mom community. So what does all of that mean? Let's identify the stages of friendship and then we'll start to talk about how we can move a friendship from one level to another.

THE ALPHABET OF FRIENDS

MBF—MIGHT BE FRIENDS: This is where friendship begins. It's the "Crossed Path" stage of friendship. You cross paths in some way—at a moms group, at church, at the park, at the library, at your kids' school—and there's a sense of intrigue, interest, or even curiosity about who they are and if you might have something in common. A friendship won't happen here, but the seed of friendship will be planted.

True friendships aren't slice and bake; they're made from scratch.

TBF—TRYING TO BE FRIENDS: This is where the seed of friendship is watered. This also might be called the "Playdate at the Park" stage of friendship. To move from MBF to TBF, you have to spend some time together and get to know one another more. In some settings this will happen automatically (at a moms group, in a work environment, at an exercise class, etc.), but much of the time this is where we have to put ourselves out there. Take a risk. Make an invite. Why? Because you can't move from MBF to TBF without showing up for time together.

GGF—GOOD GIRLFRIEND: This is where a friendship seed was planted, watered, and is now fertilized with more regular time together and deeper conversations. This might be called the "Hang in My Family Room" stage of friendship. There's a mutual enjoyment experienced when spending time together. We no longer feel the need to pick up the toys or clean the crumbs off the counter before this friend comes over. This level of friendship isn't usually experienced before you've had a handful (maybe six to eight) of TBF connections and you're feeling more and more comfortable around each other. This is the stage where you can spontaneously call and ask her to watch your kids at the last minute and she can do the same. This stage of friendship might also lend itself to setting up regular date night trades if you're married, or sanity saver nights if you're a single mom.

BFF—BEST FRIENDS FOREVER: This is the "Know Your Garage Code" stage of friendship. She doesn't knock on the door, just walks in and yells. You can laugh together and share your pain and your struggles. You know this person's strengths and her weaknesses. You can cry on each other's shoulders. This is your "call in the middle of the night friend" because there's a commitment to one another. You know this person will show up when you need her and you're committed to show up when she needs you. You're both emotionally healthy for each other, and when you are with her you are refueled and not drained. We love our BFFs like a sister. In fact, for some of us, she *is* the sister we never had or the sister we wish our sister had been. Not every friendship reaches this level, but a handful of BFFs makes your mom community even richer. These relationships, however, usually take a year or more to make. True friendships aren't slice and bake; they're made from scratch. They can't be rushed and are the result of time, vulnerability, and commitment.

Of course, relationships don't usually fit neatly into these categories. While these relationship stages have blurred lines between them and usually blend into one another without us even labeling them or realizing it, this helps us to understand the types of friends we need and the progression of friendships we will experience. Now we need the "how." Are you ready to jump in and improve your friendship-building skills?

THE DIY OF GF RELATIONSHIPS

Friendship is a Do It Yourself (DIY) project. No one can do it for you. You have to make the effort to move your relationships from MBF to TBF to GGF, and some may even become BFF. Just like we can find DIY tips and tricks in videos and articles online, and instruction sheets at your local home-improvement store, there are certain DIY tips and tricks when it comes to forging friendships.

DIY Friendship Tip #1
Look for mom friends in mom places.

Where are you scoping out potential friends (and yes . . . we all do that!)? Are you looking in the right places? In order to step into the MBF ring, we have to step outside our door and find our people! Just exactly where does a mom looking for friends find some prospects? Although many times we meet friends in unlikely environments, here are a few possible places where you can increase your chances:

Moms Groups
One of the best places to build your mom squad is by attending a moms group. Just attending a group won't net you a whole slew of friends—

you'll have to take some important steps to plant seeds of friendship (we'll talk about that in a bit). However, attending will put you in the right soil. You'll have many women to consider as friendship prospects. Many moms groups are designed for moms of infants, preschoolers, or school-age kids, but occasionally a church will have a group for moms of teens.

How do you find a moms group? One of the best places to start is seeing if there's a MOPS (Mothers of Preschoolers) or Moms Next (moms of school-age kids) in your community. Simply go to MOPS.org and click on "Find a Group." If your kids are school age through adults and you'd like to pray with other moms, you can seek out a Moms in Prayer group. Head to MomsInPrayer.org and click "find a group" to determine if there's a group in your community. Moms in Prayer also has special groups including college, grandmothers, homeschool, prodigal, special needs, working moms, military, and more.

You can also go to meetup.com and search for moms groups in your area. However, the best way is to simply ask other moms if they are aware of any local moms groups. If you're new in town, ask moms you meet at church, at the park, or at kids' activities.

Church

Joining a small group at church will also open up the possibility of building friendships. Many churches organize small groups based upon seasons of life. This opens up the possibility that you'll be in a group with others who have kids the same age as yours. Some larger churches have single-mom support groups as well.

Volunteering at church will position you side by side with others on a regular basis. If you have an infant, the church nursery "nursing mothers' room" is a great place to meet and visit with moms who are in your same season of mothering. Sunday school classes, midweek or evening Bible studies, and other church events are also great places to meet moms!

Public Library or Local Park

Most libraries have story hours for children of specific ages. Our local library even has a children's playroom. This can be a place where you can meet other parents who have kids the same age as your kids. Local parks are also places where you just might cross paths with a potential friend. We'll look at some specific strategies on how to increase the likeliness of that in just a few minutes.

Special Interest Groups

Many cities have La Leche League groups (for breastfeeding moms), Babywearing, and Moms of Multiples Groups. There are military support groups including Military MOPS. Are you an adoptive parent? Some cities have adoption support groups. Check out your local park district for mom and tot exercise classes. A simple Google search using the type of group you're looking for and the name of your city and state will net you all kinds of possibilities!

School

If your kids are going to school together, you're likely going to be hanging out with the same group of people for many years. Volunteering in the classroom when the kids are younger and volunteering to help with the band, choir, PTA, sporting events, boosters, or school musicals when they're older will help you connect with some other moms who are in the same season of mothering you're in.

If you're a homeschooling mom, homeschool support groups are a great place to meet like-minded women. You might even find a mom who would like to trade "days off" so you can each have a break once a week!

Finding MBFs (Might Be Friends)

So you've found where moms are gathering and you're ready to plant some friendship seeds. Just exactly how do you do that?

DIY Friendship Tip #2:
Don't let striking up a conversation strike fear in your soul.

Moms don't usually bite! Although many of us struggle with this particular step in meeting people. Let's get it right out there that this is scary for many of us. It's particularly difficult for someone who's an introvert. If your heart is beating wildly and your palms are sweating just reading about this "meeting people" stuff, stay with me here. It's worth grabbing hold of your courage and taking the risk! Friendship is worth it! Let's explore some very practical things you can do to reach out!

If you've read any of my other books, you might have read about being a "Here I Am" person or a "There You Are" person. "Here I Am" people walk into a room and think, *Here I am. Come talk to me. Come make me feel comfortable. Come ask me about me.* "There You Are" people walk into a room and think, *There you are! You look interesting! I think I'd like to get to know you better!* If you're a "Here I Am" person, I can promise that you will think that moms group, church event, or playgroup was the most unfriendly group you've ever been to. Certainly there are friendlier groups than others, but how *you* approach walking into a new situation will make the biggest difference.

So let's assume you walk into a room with a "There You Are" mindset. You've scoped the room and have identified someone you'd like to talk to. NOW WHAT DO YOU DO? You can do one of three things: 1) Pull out your phone and pretend to be texting someone. 2) Introduce yourself. 3) Start a conversation.

Option 1 will not move you forward in friendships so we're taking that option off the table (although it's one many of us use entirely too often!). However, both option #2 and #3 are winning strategies to plant some friendship seeds. In a group setting (moms group, PTA meeting, Bible study, etc.), the introduction most often comes first, but in a social setting (park, playground, etc.), most likely conversation will begin the interaction. This is your chance to make someone else feel fascinating! The courage you need to muster comes not from being certain you'll be seen as charming and interesting but rather in making the effort to make her feel charming and interesting. That's a different kind of risk that's just a little easier to take.

> *Connect with a comment or compliment.*

So let's break down the second and third options practically. Not everyone is confident in introductions and casual conversations. If you're not, there are some practical steps to take. First, introduction in four easy steps:

1. Smile and look her in the eyes.

2. Offer a handshake (bypass this if you're changing a dirty diaper in the moment!).

3. Say, "Hi, I'm _____."

4. After she introduces herself, respond with, "It's nice to meet you."

Now to conversation. What if you're at a place like the park or playground where you need to actually start up conversations from scratch before you ever even get to an introduction? One of the best ways to do that is to bring activities *with you* that draw kids (and ultimately moms!) *to you.* Bubbles are a great secret weapon for meeting moms. You start blowing bubbles at the park and you'll have every kid trying to catch them. Sidewalk chalk is another kid attraction that can easily result in attracting moms. Balls work well too!

Once the kids are busy playing together, you have an open door for conversation. Before you jump into asking some mom questions, it's usually helpful to comment or compliment. Comment on how kids love bubbles. Compliment her on how well her child shares, or the cute dress her daughter is wearing. You can even compliment her on a piece of clothing she's wearing that you like. Make sure the compliment is genuine and truly something you appreciate. When sincere, commenting and complimenting help break the conversation ice and prepare the way for launching into some valuable mom questions.

Dale Carnegie says, "You can make more friends in two months by becoming interested in other people than you can in two years by trying to get other people interested in you." He's right! Of course, we all know there are some people in this world who don't want to be known. If you run into one of them on your MBF journey, don't take their cold shoulder personally. It's usually about them . . . not about you (more about that later too!).

Conversations begin with a comment or compliment, but they continue when you start to seek out commonalities. That's when you start with "The Mom Questions." There are dozens of questions you could ask, and you'll find an extensive list in appendix A. However, here are just a few to get you started.

- How old are your kids?

- What are their names?

- Do you come here often?

- What neighborhood do you live in?

- Are you originally from this community?

The goal is not to just get simple answers to these questions. What you're hoping for is to find some conversation springboards in these questions. When she shares what neighborhood she lives in, you might find out it's your neighborhood, or maybe she lives down the street from someone else you know. When you ask if she's originally from this community, you might find out she's not so you can ask her where she's from and then what brought her to the community you live in. If she's from this community, you could ask her what high school she graduated from or if the city has changed much from her growing-up years. The best way to get to know someone is mining for similarities between your life and theirs. As they answer the questions and share a little of their story, share your answers along the way too. Remember to keep the focus on being more interested in them than getting them interested in you, but do provide enough back and forth for it to be a conversation and not an interrogation!

If the two of you seem to click and your kids seem to click, you now need to put DIY Friendship Tip #3 into place. In some settings (like a moms group), you know you'll likely see the person again and be able to have more conversations before moving to Tip #3, but in other settings (like the park) you may have to move quickly.

Reach out. Say hello. Be that girl!

DIY Friendship Tip #3
You have to be forward to move a friendship forward.

When you think about inviting another mom over, do you often get cold feet? Most of us do! It was my friend Karen Ehman who gave me some much-needed perspective on this in her book *A Life That Says Welcome*. She observes that "there is a huge difference between entertaining and offering hospitality. Entertaining puts the emphasis on you and how you can impress others. Offering hospitality puts the emphasis on others and strives to meet their physical and spiritual needs so that they feel refreshed, not impressed, when they leave your home."[1]

When we first moved to Bloomington, Illinois, I had a two-year-old and a four-year-old. I knew only one person, Janice. Her husband was the pastor that my husband was interning under. One Sunday morning Janice introduced me to Sue. We were standing near the church nursery after we'd both picked up our little ones. After we chatted for a while, Sue mentioned something about maybe going to the pool sometime. I told her we'd love that. We exchanged numbers and I waited a few days but didn't hear from Sue. So I decided to pick up the phone and ask her if she and her kids would like to go to the pool together. She said yes, we picked a day and time, and I had my first mom date in the new community! The next week I invited Sue and her daughter over to our house for a playdate.

Yes, I could have waited for Sue to call me. That would have been more comfortable for sure! But I chose to actively pursue friendships rather than wait for them to come to me, and I'm glad I did. Sue was a part of my mommy tribe for many years.

What's most important at the MBF stage is to trade contact information. Get some digits. Find out her Facebook name or email address. Don't let this moment go by without attempting to make sure you have a way to connect again. Then contact her to connect again! Actively pursuing feels risky, but passively waiting feels lonely. If you're serious about finding friends, you'll have to be willing to take action. It's scary for most of us to do that, but it is necessary to find friendships. Sometimes your efforts will result in a TBF (Trying to Be Friends) direction and sometimes it won't.

This is where we probably ought to talk a bit about the reality of rejection. At some point every one of us will find someone who doesn't reciprocate conversation easily, will share contact info but make no effort to reach out or respond to you, or will even "drop" you like a hot potato after making some progress in pursuing a friendship.

Finding friends requires you to move from passively waiting to actively pursuing.

When this happens, we have to remember the next friendship tip:

DIY Friendship Tip #4
A bad friendship experience doesn't make you unfriendable.

It's inevitable that you'll experience some discouraging friendship false starts. I have. Anne has. Nearly every one of us has experienced the cold shoulder at one time or another, especially in the MBF and TBF stages. Maybe you'll even have moved past the MBF and TBF stages and arrived at the GGF season of friendship, only to experience a friend distancing herself from you for what seems like no reason at all. (We'll talk about friendship breakups a little later!)

When rejection threatens to break your heart, it's important to recognize that this doesn't make you a friendship flunky. If you've been hurt in friendship, here are some principles to remember:

1) *Don't take perceived rejection personally.* There's a much bigger chance that her disinterest or distance is about her and not about you. She may be too busy, feel stretched too thin, or have her own insecurities about relationships. Resist the urge to think this is about you being unworthy of a friendship or not good enough. Nine times out of ten, it's probably not about you at all.

2) *Resist the negative self-talk.* It hurts to be rejected or suffer a setback. There's no denying that. It's certainly possible your confidence will take a hit, but your self-worth is not determined by your friendship success. Your value is based upon how God sees you and the sacrifice Jesus made for you on the cross. Relationships are always changing, but God never changes. Keep your feet planted on the solid Rock.

3) *Expect some rejection and false starts and prepare your heart for it ahead of time.* You're not a perfect match for every person you meet. Remember you're looking for mutual interest, and a one-sided friendship won't last long. If you make peace with the fact that her desire for friendship may not match your desire, and you are grateful for figuring that out sooner rather than later, it can help you see those "no" answers in a different light.

4) *Don't be afraid to ask for friendship feedback if someone you consider a GGF is pulling away.* Unfortunately, many people aren't willing to give

One of my most treasured "mom friendships" came out of a pre-school classroom. My third child was in this particular class, and another mom, Julie, had her first child in the same class. We would chat after drop-off time or while we waited in the hallway for them to be dismissed. I had just given birth to my fifth baby, and Julie (a labor and delivery nurse) was expecting her third. Julie lived farther away from the school than was convenient to go home/come back every one of those three days per week, so one day I invited her over to my house with her other child, and our little ones played together while we got to know each other. Some days, she was just coming off a night shift of delivering babies, so she'd crash on my couch for a little nap. Other days, I was exhausted from life with a newborn, so I'd take a turn to sleep. We started swapping babysitting so we could run errands. We spent HOURS talking. We discovered we had so much in common, and found we were true sisters-of-the-heart. We have shared a lot of laughs, dried each other's tears, and have cheered each other on as we've walked this mama road together. As our kids have grown and I moved farther out of town, we don't get nearly enough time together anymore, but when we do, it's such a gift. I don't' know what I'd do without my Julie-girl!—AMANDA

honest feedback, but it's always worth asking if they have any feedback that can help you improve your friendship style. If you get valuable feedback, adjust your approach on your next friendship effort.

DIY Friendship Tip #5
Meaningful conversations are more "in the moment" than "in the Messenger."

It's only since the inception of Facebook that "friend" has moved from being a noun to also being a verb. Never before have we had a tool that puts us in a perpetual MBF state as we now do with Facebook. Are these false friendships? Do they really fall into the "friendship" category at all? Do they have a place in our mom squad?

> *When we spend too much time touching screens, we have little time left for touching lives.*

Without a doubt, the inception of Facebook has changed the landscape of friendship. Intimacy now develops in both physical and digital realms. I love my online community. Many of my verb "friends" have carried me through some very hard times in my life over the past few years, which included marriage struggles, a child with mental health challenges, and my own breast cancer journey. So I believe in the value of these relationships wholeheartedly. However, I think we need to have some important context for interacting with those we've "friended." Here are eight principles for online relationships:

1) *Online friendships are wonderful places for crowd-sourcing.* Need to figure out a great place to do a getaway with your husband or trying to figure

out how to use all the extra zucchini you grew in your garden? Ask your online friends! You'll get some great ideas in a very short amount of time.

2) *Online connection can't replace in-person connection.* Online friendships may be an extension of the TBF, GGF, and even BFF relationships you already have. They can be an additional connecting point for your relationship, but they can't be *the only* connecting point for your face-to-face friendships. Be careful of the false sense of connection online association can give you. Pick up the phone, set up a playdate or a coffee date, or go for a walk with your noun friends in addition to connecting with them online.

3) *Online friendships can actually turn into GGF relationships with some extra attention.* It is possible to move from MBF, to TBF, to GGF, and I have heard of some BFFs who haven't actually met, but you have to make extra effort to make that happen. When online friendships take flight, it usually means there's quite a bit of private chatting, some occasional phone calls, emailing, and maybe even an effort to get together if one or the other of you happen to be traveling close by. An online friend can't replace your need for in-person friends who you trade sitting with or who bring you a casserole when you have a baby, but they can move through the stages of friendship and be an important part of your support system.

4. *Online relationships can rob us of the experience of being present in our face-to-face friend's life.* It's easy to get sucked into spending too many hours perusing our Facebook feed or scrolling through Instagram. This can cause us to miss out on really taking the time to talk with a friend and hear her heart or help her with something she really needs help with. When we spend too much time touching screens, we have little time left for touching lives.

5. *Online friendships can't replace in-person friendships.* Both are important but they can't replace each other. When I was experiencing horrible nausea after chemotherapy, my online friends offered wonderful words of encouragement and prayer support, but it was my in-person friend Tonya, who ran around town gathering for me all things ginger in an effort to settle my tummy.

6. *Digital sites help us to network in wonderful ways.* Online friends are found through a shared connection; one that isn't based upon location. Several years ago I formed a secret Facebook group for parents of kids with RAD (reactive attachment disorder). Because this is a situation that is unique to parenting adopted children, I knew I needed to look beyond where I live. I'll likely never meet most, if any, of the people in the group, but we all understand each other's life, share resources when we find them, and serve as a real-time support group when dealing with difficult issues.

7. *Online relationships provide intimacy without commitment.* This flies in the face of how friendships develop, are nurtured, and maintained. It's all too easy to unfriend someone when we disagree rather than talk through those differences. In her Hearts at Home book *Screens and Teens,* Dr. Kathy Koch talks about how we're growing an entire generation who don't know how to persevere. She calls the younger generation the "culture of restart," because they'd rather restart something than repair it. This comes from when our technology freezes up or has a problem and all we have to do is reboot to get back on track. Friendships can't be rebooted. They require old-fashioned, hard conversations sometimes. We have to remember that because of this, online relationships can be more easily disposable.

8. *It's easy to say something online that you wouldn't necessarily say in person.* The lack of face-to-face contact makes you bolder than you normally would be. Because you're interacting with a screen instead of a person, critical words can too easily slip through your fingers and be posted online before you even think through the consequences. It's also possible they will read your words differently than you intended for them to be received. Friendships can be damaged when you try to handle conflict through online tools. Pick up the phone, set up coffee, but do not attempt to resolve an issue through any typing tool like email, social media, or texting (we'll talk more about navigating conflict in the next chapter!).

DIY Friendship Tip #6
Keep your circle broken.

In her wildly popular blog post titled "Keep Your Circle Broken," Sara Horn shares a story that's probably all too familiar for many of us.

Stepping through the doorway, I took in the scene—cozy, comfortable rooms, a beautiful gathering space for women the church had created by refurbishing an old house on the property. I tried hard to work up my courage, trying to trust my hardest that God would help me find new friends.

Bright, bubbly women stood in clusters as groups mingle and visited. I paused, straining to see a familiar face and wondered where I should even start. Standing by myself, though, made me feel even more conspicuous so I quickly moved to the nearest half-circle of talking women and smiled my warmest greeting. "Hi, I'm Sara, how are you?"

The woman who glanced over at me returned a thin smile and offered a polite "Oh hi, glad you're here," before turning back to the ladies behind her. Another breath. Another step. I willed myself to ignore the pang in my chest while the little bit of courage I'd walked in with fizzled and sagged.

As I walked around the rooms of that little horseshoe-shaped house, I felt like a satellite, moving in my own tiny orbit. The knots of ladies talking and laughing all seemed oblivious as I moved past. Everyone looked so comfortable, so at home. Everyone but me.

I tried, again and again, to find an opening in one of their huddles. I asked questions—"How long have you been at this church?" "A long time." "Which small group do you go to?" "So-and-so's." As quickly as they began, the conversations were over.

Such perfect little circles, I thought, as I made my way out the door I'd entered just seven minutes before. *But not one with room for me.*[2]

Too often we don't stop and think about whether we're making it easy for a mom to enter into our circle of friendship. We're so focused inside the circle that we miss seeing who's outside the circle. In the same way we need to be a "there you are person" when stepping into new environments, we all need to be "there you are people" keeping an eye open for those who are new to an environment in which we're comfortable. Doing so will ensure that others are seen and valued. Making someone feel cared for doesn't commit you to friendship for life. Your friendship plate might be full, but you can still take the time and make the effort to "see" someone new and make them feel cared for. You can also help them break into the circle by introducing them to others.

WHAT'S GETTING IN THE WAY?

We've got our DIY tips under our belt, but are still having trouble with friendships.

It's possible there are some cultural changes that have affected our ability to make connections. We now have some obstacles in our way that previous generations didn't have to deal with. In order to move forward in friendships, we need to understand what might be getting in our way.

Electronics

You're sitting at the park watching your kids play when, suddenly, another mom shows up. You don't know her and don't really know what to say to her, so you pull out your phone to check Facebook, pretend to text, or flip through the same emails for the twentieth time.

While it's handy to have so much information at our fingertips, we tend to resort to it too often. If we're honest, we sometimes use our electronics to avoid the threat of uncomfortable human contact. We are overattached to technology and underattached to people. *Are your electronics keeping you from meeting people?*

Texts and Emails

Texts and emails are fabulous tools for communicating facts and information. They are not designed to be used for deep conversations or connecting at an intimate level. Sometimes we're using this wonderful tool for quick, easy communication as a replacement for important face-to-face conversations. It seems we're becoming experts at written communication and novices at real conversation.

Are texts and emails replacing valuable conversations?

Earbuds

I left the Hearts at Home office and headed to my car. The office is right in the middle of a neighborhood, so as I walked to the car I noticed our neighbor, her back toward me, was weeding the fence line between her house and our small parking lot. It was one of the first beautiful days of the spring, so I energetically said to her, "Now you've got me inspired. I need to go home and do the same thing!"

No response at all. I was caught off guard by the lack of response and first thought she was ignoring me, but then I thought she just didn't hear me so I started to speak to her again. That's when I saw the earbuds and the cords connected to the phone in her pocket. She was in her own little world, listening to music or a podcast, but absolutely closed off to any kind of connection. *Are you shutting out the world and then wondering why no one is talking to you?*

My friend was thirteen years old when she started babysitting me as a newborn. She was the coolest and most fun babysitter I had growing up. We stayed close even after she moved away for college. As I finished high school and college, we continued to stay in touch. We're both married now, have a few kids, recently moved to the same town, and are becoming more like sisters every day! —LINDSEY

Garage Door Openers

Sitting on Anne's front porch, we watched her neighbor turn onto their street. We gave a courteous wave as she pulled into the driveway. Magically, and with no need for her to exit the car, her garage door opened. She pulled the car into the garage and the door closed behind her. No opportunity for connection existed.

Garage door openers are fabulous inventions . . . particularly when it's cold and snowy. However, they make it easy for us to enter and leave our house without connecting with our neighbors in any way. *Are you making opportunities for casual conversation to happen in your neighborhood?*

Pace of Life

"Tonight one kid has a baseball game, another a swim meet, and my husband is playing basketball in the church league," said a friend I saw at the grocery store when I asked her to walk that evening. Life is often too busy to fit in some "walking and talking," or coffee, or a girls night out. The offer is sometimes there but the opportunity is lost because we've said yes to too many things.

There are more opportunities than ever for our kids, our spouses, and ourselves to be involved in. Sports, music, theater, church, clubs, social events, and all kinds of activities keep our calendars full. *Is your pace of life crowding out your space for friendships?*

Social Media

While social media has friendship benefits that we just explored, it can also be a barrier to friendship. We can experience a false sense of connection, thinking that we know what's going on in someone's life because of what they put out on social media. When in reality, there's really something else happening behind the scenes that only a face-to-face conversation might be able to tease out.

"Liking" a post isn't the same as talking about something and sorting through the feelings. Commenting can cause misunderstandings because it may be read differently than you "heard" it in your head as you wrote it. The lack of emotion in the written language makes social media a better place for information exchange than it does for heart-to-heart conversations. *Are you replacing real conversations with online connections?*

YOUR MOSAIC TRIBE

As you're putting together your mom tribe, don't discount developing friendships with women who are in different stages of life than you are. My friend Becky, who is about ten years older than I am, reminds me that there have been times she's been able to help me because she had the freedom a mom with kids still at home wouldn't have had. We need women who are in our same season of life for sure. However, we need to also be open to relationships with those who are journeying behind us and those who are ahead of us.

We've now established some categories that will help us understand different stages of friendship. We've got some DIY tips under our belt and we've checked to see if we unknowingly have friendship barriers in place. Now we need to understand all the mothering personalities out there and how to avoid some friendship frustrations along the way. We're all unique, see the world through different eyes, and have our own baggage we carry into friendship. Turn the page and let's explore the relational dynamics we have to navigate as we build a beautiful mosaic of friendship.

FROM ANNE'S HEART

*I began attending MOPS when Rilyn was six months old. I
really didn't have any "mom" friends and was craving same-
season friendship. My mom was going to be speaking at a local
MOPS group in a few months and I wanted to attend incognito
for a while. I wanted them to know me for me and not for who
my mom was. I was the only one with an infant at my assigned
table and so at times I felt like I didn't belong. I questioned
whether or not I should continue to attend, as I didn't seem to
have much in common with these women because our children
were in different stages of life. I decided to stick it out, and as
the year continued I learned a lot from these women but never
found a connection of friendship.*

*It took me three years to find my Strawberry Pink girls.
Our table just clicked, all eleven of us. We shared tears, laughter,
struggles, and encouragement. We rallied around the friend
whose husband was deployed, encouraged the friend whose husband was living and working in a different state, and supported
the friend whose son was killed in an accident. We prayed for
one another, played in each other's homes, and had girls night
outs together. These friends held me up when my dad went
through a midlife crisis and left for a few months. I had never
experienced friendship like this and was relishing in it.*

*The following year, I moved away and was brokenhearted
to leave these dear friends I had made. Facebook has been great
in keeping us connected, and several of us make attending the*

Hearts at Home conference our annual reunion. I am so grateful I stuck it out with MOPS even when I wasn't initially getting the deep connection I desired.

I've learned that connection takes time. In our "instant" society, we are often inclined to believe that great friendship happens just as fast as "Confirm" is pressed on a Facebook friend request. That's not the way it is in real life. Friendships take time to find and nurture. Then once we connect, it's both the highs and lows of life that make us better together.

SOMETHING TO THINK ABOUT:

Have you given up too easily when you didn't find instant connection with a group?

Today's Friendship Assignment

Sometimes there's such beauty in slowing down enough to write a handwritten note to someone you care about. Today take a few minutes to write a friend a note of appreciation or encouragement. If text or email is all you can do, that's better than no communication at all. However, if you can, pull out a notecard, write a heartfelt note, and put it in the mailbox.

You'll bring sunshine to your friend's day and invest in a relationship that means something to you.

## CHAPTER 3

Variety Is the Spice of Life!

One afternoon my friend Sharron and I sat in my kitchen musing about mothering personalities. As a new mom, Sharron was trying to figure out the ins and outs of mom friendships. She was doing her best not to compare herself to other moms, but finding it hard at times! We talked about how we're each wired uniquely as individuals and how that plays into our temperament and personality as a mom. We also brainstormed how those temperaments and personalities translated into differing mom styles. Before you knew it, she and I had fleshed out a future Hearts at Home conference workshop and many of the concepts in this chapter!

Psalm 139:13–14 (NIV) reminds us that we are each unique creations. "For you created my inmost being; you knit me together in my mother's womb. I praise you because I am fearfully and wonderfully made; your works are wonderful, I know that full well." So here's a question for us to consider: If we are unique creations, why do we keep trying to be like someone we're not and why do we insist that others be more like we are?

More than any other generation of moms before us, we have both the advantage and the disadvantage of being incredibly connected through social media. A 1913 comic strip called "Keeping Up with the Joneses" first introduced the concept, and the phrase that is often used, of "comparing ourselves to our neighbors as a benchmark for social class or the accumulation of material things."[1] Back in 1913, you saw the Joneses once a week at church on Sunday. These days, thanks to social media, we see the Joneses once an hour or more depending on how often you're on Pinterest, Facebook, Twitter, Instagram, and any other number of social media outlets. Our opportunity to compare has risen to unimaginable levels. The problem is that we're not making fair comparisons when we use social media and even when we interact with other moms out in public. As I addressed this challenge in my book *No More Perfect Moms*, too often we're comparing our insides to other women's outsides. We're comparing their highlight reels to our behind-the-scene reels. What we need to remember is that every mom has a backstory and a unique God-given design.

It's hard to be inspired by Christ while we're mired in self-pity.

Because we are so interconnected, it's easy to see who we aren't instead of appreciating who we are. It's also easy to see who others aren't instead of valuing who they are. First Corinthians 12:4–6 reminds us, "There are different kinds of gifts, but the same Spirit distributes them. There are different kinds of service, but the same Lord. There are different kinds of working, but in all of them and in everyone it is the same God at work" (NIV).

It's verses 15–20, though, that help us to really see both the unity and diversity in the body. "Now if the foot should say, 'Because I am not a hand, I do not belong to the body,' it would not for that reason stop being part of the body. And if the ear should say, 'Because I am not an eye, I do not belong to the body,' it would not for that reason stop being part of the body. If the whole body were an eye, where would the sense of hearing be? If the whole body were an ear, where would the sense of smell be? But in fact God has placed the parts in the body, every one of them, just as he wanted them to be. If they were all one part, where would the body be? As it is, there are many parts, but one body."

Can you see how easily we do this? We need eyes, ears, fingers, and toes—all kinds of gifts and talents—in our mom squad. Too often we whisper to ourselves, "I wish I was more _____ (organized, spontaneous, creative, etc.) like her."

Pay attention to what kind of word you would put in the blank. It's one thing to long to be more like someone from a character perspective. "I long to be more patient like she is," or "I would love to have faith like you do," are statements that can inspire us to become more Christlike. Any of the fruits of the Spirit found in Galatians 5:22–23, such as love, joy, peace, patience, kindness, gentleness, faithfulness, and self-control, are valuable for us to strive for as we draw closer to God. It's okay to see them in others and be inspired to mature in that way. However, it's hard to be inspired by Christ while we are mired in self-pity. Do you want to be more creative, more musical, more artistic, more outgoing, or more spontaneous? These are temperament and personality traits that you and I were given when God knit us together in our mother's womb. We have to embrace and celebrate who we are, resisting the urge to want to be someone we aren't created to be.

We can also use our wishing to impose how we think someone

should be. "I wish she was more _____," is a thin-veiled attempt to disguise judgment. Too easily as we relate to other moms, judgment creeps in and stains our thinking. When we can't accept the differences of others or we feel insecure when we're around someone who has a strength we don't have, our heart can easily slip into judgment.

I saw a Facebook post in my newsfeed from a mom who said her pet peeve was people wearing shoes in her house. She admitted that she didn't ask them to remove their shoes but took offense to people who wouldn't automatically do this when they came to her house. She said she didn't want the dirt and germs from shoes spread all over her house and she asked if she was alone in feeling this way. Several moms responded very strongly, "I feel the same way! How could people ever wear their shoes in the house?" or "I never wear shoes in the house! So gross!" It's not a problem to talk about these kinds of differences with other moms, but we have to keep judgment in check when we do. I responded to the post, "I do whatever people ask me to do when I go to someone's house. I won't automatically take off my shoes because we didn't do that in the family I grew up in and we don't do that at our house. You can't assume people think like you or have the same habits you do. Just ask them to do it when you greet them at the door. I'm sure they'll be happy to comply!"

We really have to be careful about how strongly we communicate our thoughts, beliefs, and habits. We have to realize our way isn't the only way. We have to understand there are other perspectives to consider.

What if we could really understand and appreciate who we are? What if we could better understand other moms and be more accepting of how they are different from us? How might that make a difference in our friendships?

For many things in life, there is no right or wrong. There's just "different." We are each a unique "style" of mom. We need to know our style, and understand both the strengths and the growth opportunities of that style.

My hope is that the pages in this chapter will help us become more self-aware. I want us to know who we are and to celebrate that fully. I also hope that you'll start seeing other moms through different eyes, resisting the urge to compare or criticize. Finally, I hope you'll be able to identify ways God might want to grow you in your personality type. Every strength we have also has a dark side. If we can be aware of these growth opportunities, it will increase our acceptance of ourselves and others, mature us in our spiritual journey, and deepen our intimacy in relationships.

Too easily as we relate to other moms, judgment creeps in and stains our thinking.

Before you read any further, I'd like you to hop over to appendix B where you'll take a short survey I call the MPI—Mothering Personality Inventory. This will help you determine your mothering personality traits that we'll discuss in the rest of this chapter. Once you know your personality traits, we'll explore how they affect your mothering and your mom friendships.

ARE YOU AN INTROVERT MOM OR AN EXTROVERT MOM?
(Personality Trait #1 from the MPI in Appendix B)

For years, I thought I was an extrovert because I'm pretty comfortable in social settings. Then I learned that I was using a wrong definition of introvert and extrovert. I thought introverts were shy and extroverts were outgoing. However, it doesn't have much to do with social strength or anxiety. Instead it's really about how you are emotionally refueled. Introverts are refueled by being alone, and extroverts are refueled by being with people. Let's look at each of these MPI traits and better understand them both.

An **introvert mom** is refueled by being alone. She enjoys the inner world of concepts and ideas. Her strengths include being content when she is alone and engaging in deep conversations. She may only have a few close friends, but she can be very satisfied with those relationships.

Her growth opportunities include needing to intentionally carve out quiet into her days (can you say rest time?), and resisting the urge to isolate herself. An introvert mom may benefit from trading babysitting with another mom on a regular basis so she can have some alone time in her own home. Being part of a Bible study, moms group, or even pursuing a hobby that requires her to spend time with others can help keep isolation at bay. Are you an introvert with an extrovert spouse or child? You'll need to balance your need for time alone with their need for being around people.

An **extrovert mom** is refueled by being with other people. She enjoys the outer world of people and things. Her strengths may include making friends easily and having a big mom community. In fact, she might not ever be without an option of someone with whom to trade babysitting! She can be a party waiting to happen.

Her growth opportunities include discovering the value of solitude. She may have to learn to draw out quieter "inner world" people . . . even her own spouse or children! She also may need to learn how to move from "wide conversations" about what she knows to "deep conversations" about what she feels. An extroverted mom may have to adjust her social tendencies in order to accommodate an introverted spouse or child's need to be alone.

What does this have to do with friendship? A lot! First, we need to understand who we are and who our friends are when it comes to refueling needs. If you're an introvert, you may have an extrovert friend who keeps inviting you to accompany her to group events when all you really want to do is to have a one-on-one coffee date with her. You're frustrated because she always wants to drag you along to be with a lot of people. You may even misread it and determine that being with you isn't enough. When the truth is, you're simply each refueled in different ways.

It's also important that we resist the temptation to criticize those who are different from us. Extrovert moms, let's stop criticizing the moms who don't want to come to every moms group activity that's planned. Introvert moms, let's stop being critical of the women who plan all of those activities of which you choose to only go to half. We need to not only offer each other friendship but also understanding.

ARE YOU AN INTERNAL PROCESSING MOM
OR AN EXTERNAL PROCESSING MOM?

(Personality Trait #2 from the MPI in Appendix B)

Internal processing moms solve problems by thinking about them. They think, think, and think some more. Often introverts, but not always, internal processors understand the value of quiet because it's needed for thinking time (that's why this internal processing mama has always

LOVED mowing the yard on our riding mower!). Another strength an internal processor may have is that she knows herself well because she is in tune with her thoughts and feelings. She also may make thorough decisions because she has thought through all angles of the decision before she announces her decision.

An internal processing mom's growth opportunities may include learning to communicate the thoughts in her head. Her husband or children may not know what she's thinking. They may not even know she is thinking about something! As an internal processor, I've had to learn to let my husband in on what I'm thinking. If I don't, I've been known to let him know what we . . . ahem . . . I mean I have decided about something he didn't even know I was thinking about! Internal processors, you may need to let others into your head and your heart. Your spouse, children, and your friends may not really know you, because you keep your thoughts and emotions inside of you. An internal processer may need to learn to stop internalizing her feelings—because only she knows what's happening on the inside. After all, feelings don't always tell us the truth. Finally, an internal processor may need to learn the value of collaborating and getting other perspectives as she creates or solves problems.

External processing moms solve problems by talking about them. They need to "hear themselves think" in order to sort through thoughts and feelings. External processors may have strong verbal skills because they use them to process life. People don't usually have to worry about knowing what an external processor is thinking because she's usually quick to let them know. Another strength is that she may make her needs known to others. I say "may" because our personalities and temperaments are all affected by our family of origin. An external processor who grew up in a home where "children are seen but not heard" may not be skilled at making her needs known because her voice was hushed for so long.

An external processing mom's growth opportunities may include learning not to monopolize conversations (particularly around internal processing mamas who need to be drawn out). She may need to learn to tell stories succinctly (not every detail is important!). My external processing daughter Erica says that she finds herself easily overwhelmed if she isn't able to process with someone. This is a place she feels she's growing to better understand herself and how her temperament affects her emotions.

How does this trait affect your friendships? First, it's important to understand how we best process and how we are similar or different from those with whom we do life. We have to resist the urge to criticize those differences. Internal processing moms, it's time to knock off the criticism of moms who talk a lot at Bible study. External processing moms, it's time to knock off the criticism of those who process internally and don't participate in moms-group/small-group discussions as much as you would like them to. After all, we can only be better together if we really understand and appreciate ourselves and the moms with whom we do life!

WHEN IT COMES TO HOME ORGANIZATION, ARE YOU AN INNIE OR AN OUTIE?

(Personality Trait #3 from the MPI in Appendix B)

I remember the day like it was yesterday. I was a young mom who had just moved to town with a two-year-old and a four-year-old. I invited my new friend Beci over for a playdate. We lived in a townhouse apartment where we had set up a playroom in the basement along with an area for storage and laundry. Beci and I headed downstairs in the storage/laundry area to gather some craft supplies to do a project with the kids. I had PILES of laundry—everywhere! That was normal for me. It obviously wasn't normal for Beci because she nearly gasped aloud and said, "Is it always like this?"

We're all different and that includes how we organize our stuff. There's no right or wrong . . . just different. If we don't understand each other, however, we can find ourselves quickly coming to wrong conclusions about each other.

Innies appear very organized because most of their stuff is "in" something. They tend to have files, not piles. Their kitchen counter is practically naked. An innie's mantra might be, "A place for everything and everything in its place." One of her strengths may be that she can find things pretty quickly (assuming she remembers the "place" she assigned something!). Innie moms may find hospitality easier because their home seems ready for hospitality at any time. The lack of clutter in their home can contribute to a sense of peace.

Growth opportunities for innie mamas might include having to deal with some control issues. Your need to organize things could cause stress for others—especially if you have perfectionist expectations. Some innie mamas don't like messes, so they may hesitate to let their kids do anything that makes a mess. Finally, when taken to an extreme, some innie mamas' families can feel like they live in a museum rather than a home.

Outies often have to deal with clutter. That's because their mantra might be, "Out of sight, out of mind!" Outies might love sticky notes and use them everywhere. (I even have digital sticky notes on my computer desktop!) They tend to be pilers rather than filers, because if they file something, they might forget about it. Their strengths may be that they are easygoing and more relaxed about their "stuff." Messes don't bother them too much. They might also be more relationship-focused than task-focused.

Growth for an outie may be coming to grips with clutter that's causing feelings of chaos in her home. This might not bother her, but it could bother a spouse or a child who is an innie living with an outie. Another challenge some outie moms face is feeling uncomfortable having people in their obviously imperfect homes. Growth opportunities for outie mamas might include having to come up with some sort of organizational system in order to find things. I'm an example of an outie mom who was bothered by the clutter caused by my outiness. I've had to learn some innie organizing principles to tackle the frustration I experienced with my piles. My organizational strategies, however, are still true to my "outie" design.

I met my bestie the winter her family moved next door to our parsonage and church. We have been best friends ever since. No person but my hubby knows me better. Our friendship has lasted through so much . . . her husband's military career moving her all over the world, our seven kids, our many moves, sickness, death, juvenile diabetes, autism, cancer, depression, happy times, memorable moments, children driving, foster kiddos, potty training, and sooo much more! We may not always be there in person for each other but we are just a call, text, or Facetime away! She is so much more than my best friend . . . she is family!
—LEANNE

How does this affect our friendships? This can be a tough one for relationships. Innie moms often can't understand how an outie mom can live in her clutter. She may judge her as being lazy or disorganized. Outie moms may feel intimidated by their friends' or neighbors' "perfect" homes. They may also be tempted to judge an innie mom on her need to relax or let the kids make messes. Then there's the whole hospitality piece.

If you want a friendship to flourish with a friend who has a different mom style than you, you may have to meet in the middle in some way.

We're going to have trouble making friends if we're hesitant to have someone in our home (either because we don't want the mess or because it's too messy to invite someone over). Yet coming to understand and appreciate our differences in how we keep our homes can go a long way in helping us link arms with one another in the mommy world.

ARE YOU A SPONTANEOUS MOM OR A STRUCTURED MOM?
(Personality Trait #4 from the MPI in Appendix B)

Every mom has a tendency to approach her day in a certain way. She's likely either spontaneous or structured or somewhere in between. We need to choose to be fascinated, not frustrated, with these mom differences. Let's look at the strengths and the growth opportunities for each of these mom personality traits.

Spontaneous moms tend to be free spirits. They live in the moment, not wanting to waste too much time planning the future. Spontaneous moms may find it easier to be "yes moms" when their kids ask them to do something like cook an egg on the sidewalk on a very hot day. (Search "yes mom" over at jillsavage.org to read that story. Hint—I'm structured, not spontaneous, so yes wasn't my first answer when my boys asked to do that!) Spontaneous moms can be fun moms. If there are puddles to be jumped through, you just might don your boots and join your kids. A spontaneous mom's home may be a gathering place for kids in the neighborhood because of the fun they can have there.

As far as growth opportunities go, some spontaneous moms struggle with procrastination and getting things done. Some admit they'd choose play over work any day. Some (not all) spontaneous mamas have trouble being the parent. She loves being fun-loving and doesn't want to make her kids sad. If you're a spontaneous mom, you may have trouble meshing with a spouse or a child who has more of a structured temperament.

Structured mamas like to have their ducks in a row. They plan and organize just about every part of their life. A structured mom's strengths include making sure appointments happen and everyone gets to wherever they need to go. Depending on where they are on the spectrum, some structured mamas have calendars and closets that are color-coded. Her kids may have many adventures because she loves to organize field trips and meaningful experiences for her family.

In terms of growth opportunities, a structured mama may struggle to play with her kids (unless it is planned!). She might also not allow enough time for kids to be kids. Some structured moms would choose work over play any day simply because of the sense of accomplishment found in work. Others are so achievement oriented that they struggle with the lack of accomplishment found in everyday mom responsibilities. Your structure might clash with your child or spouse's spontaneous temperament. You might have to let them be themselves and let go of control.

When it comes to friendships, these differences can be a huge factor. Spontaneous moms, like my free-spirit, artistic daughter Erica, can sometimes struggle to make plans with other moms because they want to reserve the right to be spontaneous with their day. Admittedly, she doesn't want to have her life run by a calendar so she's missed appointments, library story hour, and playdates as a result. On the other hand, Erica's spontaneity makes her a fun mom who gets an idea, like making felt dolls that her three-year-old can "dress," and carries it out within hours. Depending on where a structured mom is on the spectrum, she might struggle with a spontaneous friend who calls and asks if she wants to do something in an hour. If you want a friendship to flourish with a friend who has a different mom style than you, you may have to meet in the middle in some way.

Spontaneous moms, let's stop being intimidated by moms whose calendars are color-coded. Celebrate who they are and recognize that's not who you are! Structured moms, let's stop criticizing that spontaneous mom who sometimes seems more like a kid than an adult. Celebrate who she is and embrace her differences from you. Both kinds of moms make the mom world complete!

ARE YOU A MEDIUM-LOW CAPACITY MOM
OR A MEDIUM-HIGH CAPACITY MOM?
(Personality Trait #5 from the MPI in Appendix B)

It was marriage that taught me about capacity. This medium-high capacity woman married a medium-low capacity man. Of course, we didn't figure that out until after we said, "I do," and weathered a handful of conflicts. Thirty-two years and five kids later, it's interesting that every one of our kids got my husband's emotional capacity (even the adopted one—go figure!). If you think this isn't important to understand in marriage and parenting, think again. It's also a difference that can be felt, and needs to be understood, in mom circles.

What exactly is capacity? Think of a bridge that has a posted weight capacity. If a truck exceeding the capacity drives over the bridge, the bridge will crack. It's not the bridge's fault; that's how it was created. Capacity is the physical and emotional energy you have. It also may indicate how many balls you can juggle before it's too much. In navigating a recent life transition, my friend Lori shared about capacity on her blog when she said, "I often tell people that I'm built for 45 mph and my life has been 65 mph for years. I'm tired, worn out."[2]

It often seems our culture tends to value the go-getter task-oriented mentality more, but both medium-high and medium-low capacity moms are needed in the mom world. I'm a medium-high capacity mom and Anne is a medium-low capacity mom. In addressing the concept of capacity, Anne says, "I think capacity gets a bad rap. Just because I'm a medium-low capacity person doesn't make me 'less than' a medium-high capacity mom. Understanding capacity helps me understand my limits. It explains why my medium-high capacity friend (or mom!) can do five things at once and my limit is three. It helps me embrace ME!"

Anne goes on to explain how this has helped her in her friendships. She describes her friend Robyn as a medium-high capacity mom. Anne watches Robyn's kids in her home day care. When Robyn picks the kids up, she loves to visit. She gets off work and seems to be energized as she heads into the evening. Conversation seems effortless for her. Anne, on the other hand, is completely depleted at the end of the workday. An extended conversation takes more effort than what she has energy for. While Robyn would love to visit more, she recognizes Anne's capacity is different than hers and respects when Anne's medium-low capacity is maxed out. Anne says, "I'm so grateful Robyn understands our differences, doesn't take it personally, and adjusts her expectations of what it looks like when she picks up the kids."

Medium-low capacity mamas have a variety of strengths. Most understand the value of downtime. Doing-nothing time. If you're a medium-low capacity mom, you might be more "in the moment" because you're not thinking of what comes next. It's possible you are in tune with your kids' emotional and behavioral cues because you're not taking life at a Mach 2 speed. You may also experience more relaxed conversations and playtime with your kids. A medium-low capacity mom can be a good leader as long as she doesn't say yes to too many opportunities. If she has a natural creative bent, she could be a Pinterest mom because she has enough margin in her time to tackle challenging projects.

> *We should ask ourselves often, "I'm capable, but am I called?"*

Growth opportunities for medium-low capacity moms might include getting stuck in a rut because it might feel like a big deal to add something to her schedule. She might have trouble getting things done and could become easily overwhelmed. A medium-low capacity person may need a medium-low capacity life, not having too many activities to manage. She might clash with a medium-high capacity child or spouse who wants to be going and doing all the time. Understanding this part of your temperament could even be a determining factor in how many children you and your husband choose to have.

A medium-high capacity mom most likely accomplishes a lot. Her strengths include multitasking well and making her high-capacity life look easy. She doesn't wear out or quit easily but keeps persevering. She can be task-driven and love to check things off her list. Medium-high capacity moms may have a houseful of kids and her kids may be involved in a lot of activities. If she has a natural creative bent matched with her medium-high capacity temperament, she could be a Pinterest mom, unafraid to tackle even the most intimidating project and staying up past midnight to get it done (I'm a high-capacity mama with no creative bent so this part would NOT describe me!).

A medium-high capacity mom's growth opportunities may include being so task-oriented her family members don't feel valued. She could have trouble with balance and may need to remind/ask herself quite often, "I'm capable, but am I called?" Some medium-high capacity mamas hesitate asking for help because they feel it's a sign of failure. Many high-capacity moms are overcommitted or have their kids overcommitted. She may clash with a medium-low capacity child or spouse who longs for more margin in their life.

How does this affect our mom tribe? Just like the other differences, it comes down to our expectations of each other. We naturally expect others to be like we are, and if we don't understand how they might be different, we can get frustrated with one another. Let's take a moms group setting: A medium-high capacity mom may find herself frustrated because it feels like she's carrying more than her fair share of responsibility. A medium-low capacity mom may feel guilty that she can't say yes to carrying more responsibility than the one job she has within the group. Medium-high capacity moms may slip into judging a mom who does less: *Why isn't she volunteering? Helping? Why aren't her kids doing more activities?* Medium-low capacity moms may slip into judging a mom who does more: *I wonder if she ever stops? Does she really listen to her spouse and her kids? I'd hate to see her to-do list.*

Medium-high capacity moms, let's stop criticizing those who don't sign up for every field trip. Medium-low capacity moms, let's resist the urge to be intimidated by those high-capacity moms. We each need to be true to ourselves, allow others to be different, and knock off the judgment that creeps in our head and heart so easily.

DO YOU FIND YOUR TRIBE OR CREATE IT?

Once we understand the stages of friendship and the differing mom styles we have and will encounter, we're ready to assemble our mom community. So do you find your tribe or create it? The answer to that question is yes and yes. You both find and create your mom tribe.

On occasion, a mom may find a group of friends that just click. All of you enjoy each other's company, you both give and receive from one another, and you become a mom squad like none other. If you have found a sisterhood like that, thank God for your unique circle of friends. Rarely are those kinds of friendships organized intentionally. They often stem from shared life experiences like a moms group, small group, work, or church. More often they happen organically after spending long periods of time with one another in some way.

In my early mothering years, I also participated in several "mom small groups." Loosely organized through our church, this was a group of four moms who committed to spend a year together. We'd meet once every other week to study God's Word or a read a book together, share what was going on in our lives, and pray with and for one another. I learned a lot from those women and I'm grateful for our time together. Any mom can create her own small group by inviting three other moms to join her for a season of time to love on and learn from each other. Most Hearts at Home books have leader's guides in them that equip any mom to be a successful group leader.

Most moms, however, build more of a patchwork mom community. They have different friends who play different roles in their life. Their friends may come from different parts of life including church, moms group, work, or neighborhood. They may or may not know one another and they may or may not cross paths with one another.

Friendships aren't once and done either. They are fluid. Seasons of life, our transient society, changing interests, or life circumstances all keep our friendships morphing. Most of us will have relationships going in several of the friendship stages: keeping an eye open for some MBFs, a few TBFs in process, and some GGFs. A mom may or may not have a BFF, and that's okay. There may be seasons where you feel your friendship bucket is very full and you're limiting the MBFs and TBFs until you have more capacity or a change in life moves a GGF or BFF in another direction. That's okay too. You may also feel like

TBF—TRYING TO BE FRIENDS

MBF—MIGHT BE FRIENDS

GGF—GOOD GIRLFRIEND

BFF—BEST FRIEND FOREVER

you get stuck in MBF and TBF mode and rarely experience GGF relationships. That happens too. Hopefully, the shared wisdom on these pages will both inspire and equip you to invest intentionally to move some of those friendships forward.

My current mom community is very different from my mom community twenty years ago or even ten years ago. My needs are different so my friendships have changed. My three closest friends all come from different parts of my life. The four of us aren't a group. I get together with each of these women individually. When my marriage crumbled and I got my cancer diagnosis, they each brought support in their own unique way. I also have a handful off GGFs upon whom I can depend. There are some TBFs as I forge some new friendships from women I've met in my hard season of marriage and my hard season of cancer.

In the same way that we need to understand the stages a friendship goes through in the friendship-building process (remember, we don't become BFFs overnight), we also need to understand the different buckets of relationships we all have. Some of our friendship challenges may be the result of not understanding where a relationship fits in what I call the friendship frame. The closer a friend is to the center frame, the more expectations you will likely have and can have for the relationship. The farther away someone is, the fewer expectations you'll have for them. This also helps us to understand where the stages of the friendship-building process fit into the friendship framework.

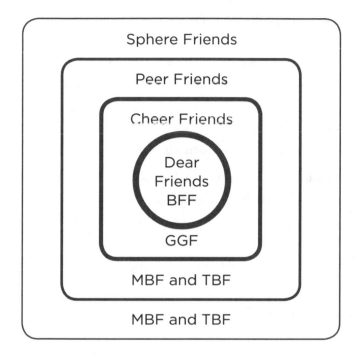

DEAR FRIENDS—This is your inner circle. Besties. BFFs. These friends supersede your season of life. They surpass the common bond that originally brought you together. I put them right in the middle box *with you* because they are doing life right *alongside you* in some way. These relationships often have the foundation of a deep spiritual connection. You pray for these gals. These are your "like family" relationships—the family you get to choose! (Family members might be part of this friendship frame if you're particularly close to your mother, sister, sister-in-law, or cousin.) You can expect them to be there for you in the good and the bad. You both make time together a priority in your life.

CHEER FRIENDS—These are the girlfriends who cheer you on in life. They help you out in a pinch and are an important part of your mom squad. You learn from them, hang with them, and care for them. If you have a mentor, she might be in this group of friends (or she might fall in your Dear Friends framework!). This is where your GGFs sit in your friendship framework. It's also where some family relationships might sit. You spend time with them as you do life together in some way or another.

PEER FRIENDS—These are your network-of-life friends. You don't usually hang with them unless circumstances bring you together. However, if you're looking for more GGFs, you might look here where there are a lot of MBF and TBF possibilities. You primarily see these friends at work, church, kids' activities, support groups, and other places where you're doing the same activities.

SPHERE FRIENDS—These are people in your sphere of life. You don't really hang with them, but you know who they are and they know who you are. They may include people you're connected to on Facebook but no other way. Old friends from high school, people who were peer friends in a past mothering season, and other acquaintances you've met along the path of life are all a part of this level of friends. You don't see them at all unless you bump into them in person or online. This is also where you'll find both MBF and TBF relationship possibilities.

Remember that friendships are fluid. Relationships move both toward the center frame and away from the center frame depending on life circumstances. This is normal. It's the natural ebb and flow of relationships. It's also important to know that some relationships may not sit neatly in one of these categories. They may be "in process" somewhere between two categories.

The importance of understanding where a friendship sits isn't to slap a label on our relationships or to feel good or bad about the relationships we have or don't have. Rather, it helps us adjust our expectations of one another. It assists us in knowing where we need to invest our relationship time. It also helps us to identify the types of friendships we need to be more intentional about pursuing.

Now that we understand the stages of building a friendship, the differing mom styles we'll bump up against, and the different levels of friends we all have in our friendship framework, it's time for us to look at the ins and outs of doing life together. What does it mean to "mom" with someone? In what ways are we really better together? Turn the page and let's dig into how God uses friends to make us better.

FROM ANNE'S HEART

My friend Robyn is so creative in her interaction with her four-year-old son. She's not afraid to suddenly become a superhero in order to redirect her son's tantrum. She's also a quick thinker and, without effort, can come up with a fun game the kids can do. One day, I found myself comparing and thinking, "I wish I was more like that in my parenting." I even experienced some guilt in not being able to improvise like her. Then suddenly, as if God tapped me on the shoulder and whispered into my soul, that thought was replaced with, "You are both fearfully and wonderfully made."

With that gentle reminder, God moved my heart in a new direction.

God created Robyn to roll with the punches and me to be more methodic. Her distraction default balances my discipline default. Her spontaneity and creativity is what makes her such a good friend for me. She inspires me to think outside my box, and being around her makes me a better me!

My friend Emily hosts incredible Pinterest-worthy parties. She runs with a theme—right down to the water bottle label. While I love hosting parties, my creativity capacity doesn't extend past the cake and invitations. It's easy to begin the comparison game and feel inadequate, but it's in those moments that I have to start the internal work of standing in God's truth that we're both fearfully and wonderfully made.

As moms, its easy to compare ourselves to those around us. We're drawn to those who have different strengths and talents than we do. Instead of comparing and feeling we don't measure up, we need to think about how those moms complement our strengths and talents. They fill our gaps, expand our world, and play an important role in our mom tribe.

SOMETHING TO THINK ABOUT:

Do you have a friend whose natural strengths make you feel guilty? Can you turn that around in your mind, embracing her differences and seeing what they bring to your life?

Today's Friendship Assignment

I used to tell the moms in my Mom To Mom group, "Mom To Mom is where you will meet moms. Your living room is where you will build friendships." You have to make moves to build your team (and if you're not comfortable inviting someone to your living room, you can meet them at a park or a coffee shop. Stop making excuses!).

Call or text a friend (or a TBF) to set up a time to get together in the next week.

If you don't get a response or she's not willing to set up a get-together, try someone else!

Don't stop until you get a mom date on the calendar!

## CHAPTER 4

Learning Together
"What a great idea! I can't wait to try that out!"

It was my friend Doris who inspired me to wear lipstick. Kendra introduced me to the "Glorified Brownies" recipe that became a family favorite (until we all stopped eating sugar!). Becky introduced me to the Taco Stew recipe I've made for years. Our family's pumpkin bread recipe came from my friend Mindy. Crystal inspires me to be creative when organizing things. She also has a great eye for decorating and has helped me redecorate a few rooms using items I already had. Lora helped me sponge-paint the stairway and hallway walls in our home. Truly, my life, home, food, and habits have been greatly influenced by my circle of moms!

One of the biggest benefits of having a tribe is being able to access the strengths of other moms to fill in your gaps. Certainly social media, particularly Facebook, Pinterest, and Instagram, has widened the concept of sharing ideas, but there's still nothing better than learning something from a friend who has knowledge or experience you need.

We gain so much just doing life side by side. That's how I learned to fold T-shirts so you can see what's on the front of the shirt in the drawer. My friend Sue was over for a playdate and I folded a load of laundry during the visit. She picked up a T-shirt and folded it so the graphic on the front was visible. I said, "Show me how to do that!" I've been folding them that way ever since!

Anne has become passionate about natural cleaning methods and removing chemicals from her home. She began researching different methods online and found some great ideas that kick-started the process. However, it wasn't until another mom shared her journey of removing chemicals that Anne learned the most. She learned how to clean her home with vinegar and baking soda and got the idea to cut up her husband's old T-shirts to use as rags.

Recently, Anne and her husband made the decision to homeschool. While Anne was homeschooled her seventh-grade year, she never thought she would be a homeschooling parent. Overwhelmed at the thought of this new venture, she found encouragement from her friends Kesha and Genae. She gleaned wisdom and local resources from Christene. As she launches into her first year of homeschooling, she is learning from other homeschooling moms in her tribe.

I did the same during our different seasons of homeschooling. My friend Julie, who had three daughters the same ages as my three older kids, decided to homeschool at the same time. We shared many resources with one another, even banding together for weekly science lessons. Several years later, when Mark and I decided to homeschool Erica her junior and senior years, it was another mom who told me about the dual credit program at our local community college. Erica completed her high school education taking courses at the college, earning both high school and college credit at the same time! I would have never known about that possibility if it wasn't for another mom who taught me the ins and outs of homeschooling a high schooler!

Not only can we do life side by side, but we can band together to lighten the load for everyone. Every mom needs childcare for a date night; every mom needs to feed her family; every mom needs to go to the grocery store and clean her house. While most of those things are thought of as solitary activities, there are ways we can actually help one another and even learn from each other. Setting up a regular schedule to accomplish some of these with a friend can increase the probability of them happening and increase the joy in doing them!

Over the next few pages, you'll find suggestions for doing life together in a variety of ways. Any time we mom together, we usually learn something along the way. If any of these co-op ideas resonate with you and you want the details on how to make them happen, hop over to appendix C and you'll find what you need to get started.

COOK FOR A DAY, EAT FOR A MONTH

I was first introduced to once-a-month cooking when we offered a workshop on the concept at one of our Hearts at Home conferences. I loved the idea of partnering with a friend and cooking for a day in order to have a month's worth of meals in the freezer. When the kids were small, once-a-month cooking made my life so much easier! It usually required one long day of cooking with a friend or two, but the conversation and laughter balanced out the hard work of food prep, washing dishes, and assembling so many meals. Not only did I take home a month of meals, I almost always learned food-prep tips and tricks from the moms I cooked with that day!

Another option for sharing cooking responsibility is to organize a freezer meal co-op. This is where a group of moms (usually five to eight) each make one recipe a month, but they make that recipe for each member of the co-op. So if there are eight people in the co-op and my recipe for that month is meat loaf, I make eight meatloaves. When the group comes together to swap meals, they plan the next month's recipes.

I didn't want to leave a screaming baby with my friend because I was afraid it would affect our friendship negatively.

I've also done Christmas cookie baking days with different friends over the years. We divide up the shopping list and set aside a day to bake, talk, and taste. We not only accomplish something we both want to accomplish, but we get to spend time working side by side, sharing stories, laughing, and often learning together.

MANY HANDS MAKE LIGHT WORK

I remember when my moms' small-group leader made the suggestion for Serving Saturdays. I was so excited at the thought of serving one another! Then I realized the implication for me personally—this meant I would have one Saturday I'd be on the receiving end. I was all in!

There were four of us in the group. We had committed to spending one year together. We met every other week, learning from each other, learning from God's Word, and praying together. In addition to our bi-weekly group times, we also had slumber parties, girls night outs, and now we were introduced to Serving Saturdays.

We found four Saturdays we could each commit four hours to. Then we assigned one of us to each of those Saturdays. When it was our day to be served, we had three friends for a four-hour time span to help us accomplish a project or set of tasks we wanted to get done! One of the girls had us wash all the windows in her house. Another had us help her paint a room. The third one wanted to "spring-clean" her house. I chose to have help with yard work and planting all my patio flowerpots. We all checked off several tasks on our to-do lists, but the best part was getting the jobs done faster than we could have alone and having so much fun doing them together! We laughed, told stories, and learned from each other as we worked side by side.

We did something similar in our couples' small group several years later. What a difference it makes to have help with a task that's hanging over your head! However, you don't need a small group to make this happen. You can simply form your own "Home Project Co-op"! Just gather a few friends (no more than three to five is best) and set up dates for serving each other. Decide on the time frame you'll commit to each serving session based upon availability. It doesn't require a full-day commitment so even if you choose Saturdays and there are soccer games every Saturday morning, you can still find three or four hours to commit to on a Saturday afternoon.

I'LL WATCH YOUR KIDS IF YOU'LL WATCH MINE

Mark and I moved away from grandparents, aunts, and uncles when our oldest daughter was just two years old. On a very limited budget, we made our home off-campus in married student housing as Mark pursued a ministry degree. Because we didn't have the money to pay a babysitter, we quickly learned the value of trading sitting with other couples.

Childcare trades provide more than financial benefits. Having an experienced mother watching your kids rather than an inexperienced teenager provides a sense of safety and security. Trading sitting builds a sense of community and strengthens your relationship with another family. These regularly scheduled playdates can also foster friendships for both kids and parents. If the kids play well together, even the couple doing the childcare can feel a sense of relief while their kids play with their friends.

Before we had our third child, we were trading date nights with Larry and Marianne. Our two kids were close in age to their two kids and they all played very well together. Larry and Marianne decided their family was complete with two kids, but ours kept growing. When our third came along and was terribly colicky, I told Marianne they probably ought to find someone else with whom they could trade. I didn't want to leave a screaming baby with my friend because I was afraid it would affect our friendship negatively. She said to me, "Jill, you handle Erica's screaming for hours every day. Don't you think I can handle it for two hours every other week? Plus you and Mark need some time for just the two of you in this stressful season." She was right, and I was grateful for both her wisdom and her serving heart. I would never have left my colicky girl with a teenager, but I knew Marianne had the wisdom, patience, and servant heart to make it work.

For date nights, we would find a couple, like Larry and Marianne, who had kids about the same age as our kids. We then set up a regular date night schedule for both of us. We'd watch their kids one Friday night and they'd watch our kids the next Friday night. We knew quite a few couples in our church and community who made this arrangement with one another. Two very smart couples we knew set up their dates with an overnight component. One week they watched their friends' kids from 5 p.m. on Friday until noon on Saturday. The next weekend they had their date from 5 p.m. Friday until noon on Saturday when their friends returned the favor. Each couple had a "getaway" in their own home without any expense!

Anne knows three families who do a Date Night Co-Op. On the second Friday of every month, one family babysits and the other two couples have their date nights. With this pattern, each couple has two date months in a row and then they provide the childcare the third month. It's a version of a date night swap, but with three couples instead of two.

> *I* met my BFF because our husbands grew up together. We had just moved back and started to go to church. Well, she needed someone to watch her nine-year-old stepdaughter during the day and knew I stayed at home with my girls! Slowly we started becoming better friends and now are BFFs.
> —Amanda

Exchanging sitting not only works for couples, but it can work for moms too. A single mom trading with another single mom can give both moms some much-needed respite. I know two single moms who did this for years. Every Friday night they had "junk food night" where the moms spent the evening together. They ate popcorn, pizza, or whatever was easy or sounded good (this is why they dubbed it "junk food" night). This built a sense of family between these two women and their kids.

Then on Saturday, they traded "time off" so each mom could have a little "me" time. What a gift these women were to each other. They really understood the concept of "doing life together." What did it take to start the ball rolling? One mom approached the other mom and made the initial invitation to do dinner on Friday night. They enjoyed it so much they did it the next week, and the week after that. Then one of them suggested the next step of trading "time off," and before they knew it their friendship blossomed and they laughed, learned, and lived life together.

One neighbor told Anne, "I've lived in my house for fifty years and I've never met any of my neighbors!"

My friend Mindy and I did the same thing when we were both stay-at-home moms. We traded "days off." Setting up a regular schedule assured our kids of a time to play together each week and it guaranteed us a time of respite each week. When we dropped off or picked up the kids, we almost always spent time talking, laughing, and learning. In fact, one afternoon when I came to pick up the kids from Mindy's house, she had just finished making a batch of pumpkin muffins for their afternoon snack. After the kids had their snack, Mindy and I sat down to have a muffin and visit. Those muffins were so yummy I asked for the recipe! That was twenty-five years ago and we still make those muffins today! Mindy and I were friends for a season—we stay connected on Facebook these days but don't see each other on a regular basis. I'm grateful God allowed our paths to cross when we both needed it most!

LET'S DO WHATEVER PROJECT WE'RE DOING . . . TOGETHER!

I don't know about you, but I always seem to have a project in my head that I would like to get done but never find the time to do. Anne's MOPS group hosted several Craft Nights. Each woman could bring her own project to work on or choose to do the "project of the night" that someone had organized. These girls nights out were very popular and Anne particularly loved going around Christmastime. She got the chance to work on Christmas presents, learned all kinds of things from the conversations going on around her while enjoying some much-needed "me" time. They even organized a blanket-making project for a children's shelter for women who wanted to attend but either didn't have a project to work on or just aren't particularly crafty.

A Craft Night is a simple activity to pull together with some friends! Simply send out a Facebook message to a few friends and figure out a time and place to meet up with your own projects in hand. If you don't have the space in your home, you can find a community space or ask your church if you could use a room.

EXCHANGE PARTIES

You know that vase that you just aren't excited about anymore? Or the dress in the back of your closet that you never wear? Why not host an Exchange Party with your friends? This is when you bring slightly used items to someone's house and everyone gets to walk away with new items for their house.

This was how Anne's friend Melissa discovered the perfect piece to go on her coffee table. It takes little to no effort and you can get some great tips from your friends for how to use a certain item all while enjoying a girls night. The possibilities are endless: baby gear swap, jewelry swap, book swap, children's clothing swap, craft supply swap, or home décor swap. This is a great way to help each other out and find inspiration from other moms!

GET MOVING TOGETHER

It was my friend Sue and her husband, Tom, who invited us to play sand volleyball one summer. Karen and I met a couple mornings a week to push strollers and walk. Crystal and I signed up for a "lean body boot camp" class together. We drove to class together, which provided much-needed accountability to roll out of bed and be at class by 5:15 a.m. three mornings a week! When we get moving together with a friend, it gives opportunity for conversation, inspires idea sharing, and provides accountability to take care of ourselves! Our friends inspire us, teach us, and help us be our best!

MAKING THE WORLD A LITTLE SMALLER

When a job change took Matt and Anne to a new city, they tried to make connections with their neighbors but weren't having much success aside from one or two of them. Anne says, "No one seemed interested in the act of neighboring. So we decided to host a block party! We created an invitation and knocked on each door of the neighbors on our block to personally invite them."

They considered their block party a success when, out of twenty-five houses, they had eleven represented. They learned about one another's families and learned a little bit of history about the neighborhood. Anne explained, "Several of our neighbors have lived here for close to fifty years and they kept telling us how wonderful it was to get together and that no one had ever done anything like this." One neighbor even told Anne, "I've lived in my house for fifty years and I've never met any of my neighbors."

Being intentional about fostering relationships in your neighborhood is a benefit for you and your neighbors! Have you ever considered hosting or organizing a block party? Something as simple as an intentional gathering of neighbors can make your neighborhood a better place to live.

FROM ANNE'S HEART

Have you ever noticed that Barbie dolls lose their shoes minutes after being out of the box? At least in our house they do. On one of my Pinterest perusals, I happened across a pin that suggested you hot-glue their shoes on. I sat dumbfounded. Duh! What a great idea! You better believe that the hot glue gun and I became fast friends. I went on a hot glue gun free-for-all as I glued together every toy that is supposed to stay together but always comes apart. I shared that with my mom one day and she exclaimed, "Why didn't I think of that twenty-five years ago?"

Social media is an amazing tool for learning how to do something new or gleaning wisdom from someone who has been there and done that. I am so grateful for the person who painted her curtains and blogged about the mistakes she made and what she would have done differently. It saved me from having to deal with those issues when I painted stripes on mine (I love them! They're bedsheets . . . another thank-you to Pinterest!).

I am an outie just like my mom. If I don't see it, I forget about it. However, I am still working on how to make my "outie" more "innie." I have files ready to be used for all of my paper-work; I just don't think to use them. After searching for a lost shoe for the hundredth time when she came to pick up her son from my day care, Monica exclaimed, "You need lockers for each kid!" Monica is an innie. God has gifted her with incredible organizational skills and she just has a vision for how to establish order and routine.

She recently started her own organizing business and offered her services to me. To be honest, for a brief moment I felt inadequate. However, I quickly chose to respond with gratitude and a "Yes please!" I moved from nearly feeling offended to recognizing the opportunity that was being given to me. I don't know for sure, but I'm assuming it took some courage on Monica's part to even put it out there.

That's the beauty of learning together in this motherhood journey. We get to share our experiences and knowledge with one another to make life more enjoyable for ourselves and our family.

SOMETHING TO THINK ABOUT:

Has someone offered to help you with something and you viewed it as an offense rather than an opportunity? If you receive an offer like that in the future, could you view it as the opportunity it is?

Today's Friendship Assignment

What are you doing alone that you could be doing with a friend?

Is there any kind of co-op you could organize to help share the load in some way?

(Hop over to appendix C to get yourself started!)

## CHAPTER 5

Helping Together
"You don't have to do that alone. I'll help you!"

W hen I received the invitation to the graduation party, I looked at the calendar, hoping the day would be free. It was. I called my friend Lisa, whose daughter was the graduate, and told her I was available to help her. "What do you need done? Help with setup? Serving food? Cleanup?" She said, "Thank you so much! If you're really okay with helping, I'd love some help keeping the drinks stocked." I replied, "I'm your girl. Got it covered."

Lisa has helped me many times over the years. I was gone on the weekend her oldest daughter was married and hated not being able to help, but I was glad I was available to help with her youngest daughter's graduation party. As we discovered just a few pages ago, there's so much we can learn from each other. When you add in helping each other, you've just made your world bigger and your life richer.

Let's be honest, though, offering help and asking for help isn't always the easiest thing for a mom to do. Too many of us hesitate to offer help for fear of "imposing," feeling like we don't have anything to offer, or not really knowing how to best help. We hesitate to accept help because we don't want to be a burden or we don't want to appear like we can't handle things on our own. I'm glad neither Lisa nor I got hung up on worrying about what each other thought. I offered and she accepted and both our lives were better because we did it together.

Yet that's not what always happens. Many times our insecurities and assumptions keep us from engaging in each other's lives. We don't understand the power found in the give-and-take of relationships. We let fear, self-sufficiency, and self-doubt rob us of the beautiful gift of doing life together. In fact, most of us have to push through the fear of something to experience the fullness of friendship. Let's start there.

WHEN FEAR GETS IN THE WAY

A Facebook friend shared with me a time when two of her friends were there for her:

> There was the day I found out my husband had been having an affair. When I saw my girlfriend very soon after that, I couldn't stop crying. My eyes were swollen, I couldn't see, and I was obviously heartbroken. My friend only asked one question: Want to get a hot fudge sundae?
>
> The next week, she and another friend ambushed me. At the time we were all stay-at-home moms with five kids under the age of four between us. One friend stayed with all the kids while the other took me to get my nails done and have lunch. When we came

home I discovered dinner had been cooked for my family and all my laundry was done.

Their acts of love spoke volumes to me. However, what meant even more than that was they never asked what had happened. They simply loved on me and my family and let me know they were there when I was ready. Never in my life have I felt so totally loved in a very dark moment.

"They simply loved on me and my family and let me know they were there when I was ready."

What a beautiful picture of what helping one another looks like. But what if this mom's friends were afraid to help? What if they were afraid they would appear pushy or would be sticking their noses into someone else's business? How would they have missed out on loving well?

I had a hunch that fear is one of the biggest blocks to doing life together. A simple question posted on my Facebook page confirmed that in a huge way. I asked, "What role, if any, does fear play for you in offering, accepting, or asking for help from a friend?" Here are some of the responses I received:

- I'm afraid to be seen as a "taker" or to impose on others.

- I don't want to settle for a mediocre job.

- I'm afraid to ask for help because I then feel like a failure as a wife and/or mother that I couldn't do it myself.

- I'm disappointed when it's offered but not delivered; then I'm afraid to ask again because I must be a bother.

- I'm afraid that they will keep some kind of score and I won't be able to repay the favor and make them feel used, which may limit their desire to help others in the future . . . I'd rather they save their goodwill for someone more worthy of it.

- I'm afraid of "bothering" someone and not living up to someone's expectations of me.

- I do not want to feel indebted to any human. I always want to give my time or what God has given to me to others, but it is very difficult for me to accept something from others.

- I feel like there's just not enough of me to go around. Once I care for my husband and kids, there's not much left for someone else.

- I'm afraid of what others might think of me.

- I'm afraid of failing them in some way.

- I'm afraid of being overbearing or perceived as a know-it-all.

- I'm afraid of rejection, or that they will be "too busy" to help out.

- Knowing everyone is super busy and feeling like even though they may want to help, it won't be convenient for them. Also, feeling like they will say yes only because they feel guilty saying no.

- I'm afraid of being judged and feeling like I am a failure.

- I'm afraid to offer help because I'm so forgetful that I don't want to commit to something I might forget to do!

Can you relate to any of those fears? John 10:10 reminds us that "the enemy comes to steal, kill, and destroy." His targets include marriages, families, and friendships. We have too much to lose to keep on believing Satan's lies. Let's look at a few of these false assumptions and see if we can put them to rest once and for all.

I'm afraid to be seen as a taker. We're designed to live in community with one another. In Genesis, after God created Adam, He stated, "It is not good for the man to be alone" (2:18 NIV), right before He created Eve. Those words are often associated with the marriage relationship, but they apply to any relationship. Thousands of years later, when Jesus came to this earth, He didn't do life alone. He was in a beautiful "give-and-take" relationship with His friends Mary, Martha, Lazarus, and those we know as the disciples. You and I are designed to be both givers and takers in this world.

I don't want to impose upon others. If you ask for help and someone offers to help you, you are not imposing upon them. They are choosing to give their time to you. Exercising generosity is an important part of flexing our giving muscles. Others can benefit from giving if you ask for help, on occasion.

> *You and I are designed to be both givers and takers in this world.*

I don't want to settle for a mediocre job. It's okay to want to do something well, but sometimes we need to really evaluate our motives and desires and determine if our expectations are unrealistic. If we need help and we want to do the job well, we can ask a friend who's a conscientious worker and take the time to give clear instructions. Maybe your fear is that no one else can care for your child as well as you can. Guess what? You're right! But can they care for them well for a short period of time? Absolutely! Asking for help can help you come to terms with the control issues that rob you of so much joy.

I'm disappointed when it's offered and not delivered. I don't want to ask again because I don't want to be a bother. When we intermingle our life with the lives of others, we do risk being let down. There's no way around that. At some point a friend will disappoint you and, because you're an imperfect human, you'll disappoint a friend. Our response is key to handling this well, though. Being disappointed happens, but assuming you're a bother isn't a helpful response. A friend who doesn't follow through either 1) doesn't know how to say no when she needs to say no, 2) has too much on her plate to follow through on her commitments, 3) isn't a woman of her word, or 4) may have had the best of intentions but forgot to put it on her calendar! She may feel bad she had to let you down and may really want another opportunity to help you. Give her the benefit of the doubt. None of those have anything to do with you. Don't make them about you. It's in times like these that Satan can so easily get a foothold in your head and heart to destroy. He wants to steal and destroy your friendships. Don't let that happen.

I'm afraid to ask for help because then I'll feel like a failure. What life experience taught you that lie? Who insinuated to you that if you ask for help, you fail? Most of us who believe that asking for help equals failure have some drive toward perfection. Sometimes these lies come from our family of origin or some experience in our life where unrealistic expectations were placed on us. Say this after me: *Normal people ask for help. It's okay not to know how to do something. It's also okay to realize a job can be done quicker or better with help. And it's perfectly okay to ask for help just because you don't want to do the job alone and you'd rather do it with a friend.*

I'm afraid they'll keep some kind of score; I don't want to feel indebted to someone. Granted, friendship is a give-and-take relationship, but no healthy relationships keep score. If you find yourself feeling resentful toward a friend, it could be that you are keeping score. There's a lot you can't track in relationships and keeping score is sweating the small stuff. If you're worried about them keeping score and feeling like you "owe" them something, just make sure the issue isn't a selfishness issue on your part (you don't want to give back in some way). Of course, if a relationship is all give or all take, it's not a healthy relationship at all and may need to be evaluated.

I'm afraid there's not enough of me to go around. As busy moms, I think most of us can feel this way at one time or another. Some seasons of motherhood are just plain hard. Too often we think something will be harder than it actually is or require more of us than it actually does. What you can offer to a friend needs to fit within your time and talents. Don't hesitate to "guide" a friend to what you can do: "I need someone to watch the kids next Tuesday while I go to the doctor. Could you help me out? In exchange, I'd be happy to bring you a freezer meal for your dinner that night." It's also important to remember that there are some seasons where you'll take more than you give and other seasons where you give more than you take. Don't try to make it "fair" in your mind. The ebb and flow of life doesn't work that way.

I know everyone is busy and I know that even if they want to help, it won't be convenient for them. Stop saying no for people. When you say no for someone, you talk yourself right out of relationship with them. Share your need and then let them say yes or no for themselves. There are many moms out there longing to connect with another mom and feel needed by someone. When you don't ask, you rob others of the blessing of giving.

I'm afraid to help because I'm afraid of being judged and not measuring up to their expectations. Could you let someone down by not helping them the way they wanted you to help? I suppose you could, but it's not likely. Instead, it's highly likely that your offer of help will bless her socks off! Don't let the fear of judgment rob you of the joy of giving. Let Colossians 3:23 guide you: "Work willingly at whatever you do, as though you were working for the Lord rather than for people" (NLT).

One Facebook friend who has successfully pushed through her fears said, "I used to fear asking for help until someone told me that by not asking I took that blessing away from them. Wow, that hit me so hard. I've found if I ask for help, it strengthens the bond I have with that person." She's right!

TBF—Trying to Be Friends
MBF—Might Be Friends
GGF—Good Girlfriend
BFF—Best Friend Forever

Too often our fears are keeping us from moving a TBF relationship into the GGF stage for friendship. Fear is a reason, but it's no excuse.

My friend Jody says, "Sometimes you just have to speak up!" When Jody was getting ready to move out of town, all the packing she had to do was so time-consuming. She kept thinking about the friends she would miss and how much she'd rather be with them than all those boxes. Jody was confined to her house working alone when what she *really* wanted was valuable one-on-one time with friends before leaving town. After grappling with her dilemma for a few days, she decided to ask for what she wanted. She let a friend know she could just sit and enjoy a cup of coffee while Jody did the work because she just wanted time with her! After their wonderful visit, Jody posted on social media how much she'd loved the simple company of a friend while she packed. She was amazed at the response and her calendar quickly filled with visits from different friends. Some jumped in and helped her pack and others simply visited with her while she packed. Even the visits were helping because those friends kept Jody company while she packed!

Are you making your fears bigger than your God? Come on, girlfriends, it's time to get past this stuff. We're better together when we're helping one another!

WASH SOME FEET . . . OR SOME DISHES!

"Let each of you look not only to his own interests, but also to the interests of others." These words from the Bible (Philippians 2:4) provide direction for how we are to balance our needs with the needs of others. I also love how Hebrews 13:16 in *The Message* offers encouragement about helping others: "Make sure you don't take things for granted and go slack in working for the common good; share what you have with others. God takes particular pleasure in acts of worship—a different kind of 'sacrifice'—that take place in the kitchen and workplace and on the streets."

Jesus modeled serving and sacrifice in so many ways, but it's His story of washing the disciples' feet that rocks my world every time I read it:

> Just before the Passover Feast, Jesus knew that the time had come to leave this world to go to the Father. Having loved his dear companions, he continued to love them right to the end. It was suppertime.

The Devil by now had Judas, son of Simon the Iscariot, firmly in his grip, all set for the betrayal.

Jesus knew that the Father had put him in complete charge of everything, that he came from God and was on his way back to God. So he got up from the supper table, set aside his robe, and put on an apron. Then he poured water into a basin and began to wash the feet of the disciples, drying them with his apron. When he got to Simon Peter, Peter said, "Master, you wash my feet?"

Jesus answered, "You don't understand now what I'm doing, but it will be clear enough to you later." Peter persisted, "You're not going to wash my feet—ever!"

Jesus said, "If I don't wash you, you can't be part of what I'm doing." "Master!" said Peter. "Not only my feet, then. Wash my hands! Wash my head!"

Jesus said, "If you've had a bath in the morning, you only need your feet washed now and you're clean from head to toe. My concern, you understand, is holiness, not hygiene. So now you're clean. But not every one of you." (He knew who was betraying him. That's why he said, "Not every one of you.") After he had finished washing their feet, he took his robe, put it back on, and went back to his place at the table.

Then he said, "Do you understand what I have done to you? You address me as 'Teacher' and 'Master,' and rightly so. That is what I am. So if I, the Master and Teacher, washed your feet, you must now wash each other's feet. I've laid down a pattern for you. What I've done, you do. I'm only pointing out the obvious. A servant is not ranked above his master; an employee doesn't give orders to the employer. If you understand what I'm telling you, act like it—and live a blessed life." (John 13:1–17 THE MESSAGE)

Jesus never asks us to do something He wasn't willing to do Himself. Before He modeled sacrifice in death, He modeled sacrifice in life. In Bible times, it was common practice to wash feet because they wore sandals and the roads were dusty, but also because of something else. I love the way one of my favorite fiction authors, Tessa Afshar, explains it:

> The town I live in used to be rural, with lots of farmland and fruit orchards. Some of that land is still cultivated, and you can enjoy fresh fruit and produce from town. We also have a few horse farms and our residents like riding. Once the weather turns pleasant, horseback riders are a common sight on the country roads. They often leave a steamy, rather pungent gift behind them, and you have to be careful where you step.
>
> In the glaring absence of Fords, Subarus, and Toyotas during Jesus' day, what they had a lot of was oxen, horses, donkeys, camels, and asses. In addition, flocks of sheep were moved from country paddocks into the city for sale. Not to put too fine a point on it, there was a lot of poop on the road. Carts would unintentionally spread the goods around to make sure the walking citizenry didn't miss their chance at stepping on some aromatic treasure.
>
> Even if you had just left one of the Roman baths, all clean and shining with perfumed oils, by the time you arrived home, your sandaled feet would be already filthy. Because your feet weren't merely dirty with the dust of the road, cleaning them was considered a truly nasty job, relegated to slaves.

You can imagine how incredible it was when Jesus wrapped a towel around His waist and knelt down to wash His disciples' feet. He was choosing to wash the dirtiest part of them, the most disgusting, off putting, smelly part of them. The astonishing thing is that He hasn't stopped doing that. He is still looking for our smelliest, dirtiest bits; He is still kneeling down before you and me and washing away, until He calls us clean.[1]

What a beautiful example of serving that is for us. Personally I've never washed any of my friends' feet, but I have washed a sink full of dishes. I've also washed out a friend's kitchen cabinets when she was moving into her house, and I've cleaned another friend's bathrooms when she was moving out of her house. I've had friends wash my sink of dishes, help with laundry, and scrub my kitchen floor when I was recovering from having a C-section, overwhelmed getting ready for a graduation party, or dealing with nausea from cancer treatments. We're designed to link arms with one another and live life together. In order to do that, however, we have to be willing to both give and receive help. And that's where we struggle.

THE RESPONSIBILITY OF RECEIVING

I was waiting to be taken back for surgery. Five weeks earlier, I'd heard four words no woman wants to hear: You have breast cancer. They allowed me to keep my phone with me through several hours of presurgical procedures. As I was being wheeled from one procedure to the next, I received a text from my friend Sue. She was quite ill and asking for prayer after being admitted to the hospital. I immediately prayed for her and texted back that I would continue. I told her I was doing a lot of lying around that day so I would be her biggest prayer warrior throughout the morning. I continued to pray for her until they took me back to surgery.

Sue ended up being quite ill for the entire time I was undergoing my treatment. Over the span of six months, I had surgery, chemotherapy, and radiation, and she had one procedure after another. We texted each other a lot and became prayer partners through our shared health ordeals. I had chemo treatments every three weeks, which put me on a "one bad week, two good weeks" cycle. On my bad weeks, I was pretty much nonfunctional so I was grateful for the meals friends generously brought my family.

Sue wasn't so lucky. She didn't have any cycle of good/bad weeks. All of hers were bad. On one of my good weeks, I was preparing dinner for my family. I had more food than we needed so I sent Sue a text and asked if anyone was bringing dinner tonight for her and her family. Her "no" answer confirmed God's nudging on my heart to take her a meal. I finished making dinner for both of our families, threw on my wig, and headed out the door to drive the three miles to her house.

If you struggle receiving help from friends, you likely struggle receiving help from God.

I have never been so happy to take someone a meal! Why? Because I desperately needed to give. I was on month three of receiving. Dozens of meals had been sent my way after surgery and chemo (radiation hadn't even started yet!). I was so grateful, but I desperately needed to be on the other side of the equation. Sue had to be willing to receive for me to experience the joy of giving.

Being on the receiving side of giving is hard for many of us. We don't want to be a bother. We don't want to put someone out. Deep down many of us hesitate asking for help or receiving help because we don't want to appear weak, needy, or incompetent. And that, my friend, is pride.

Most of us wouldn't think of rejecting help or hesitating to ask for help as a pride issue, but that's because it's carefully disguised as self-sufficiency. Our human nature sees self-sufficiency as a strength. If you think about it, it starts around the age of two when a child first tells her mama, "I do it myself!"

Pride denies need. Humility acknowledges need. There's a really big reason why we need to address this in our heart: If you struggle receiving help from friends, you likely struggle receiving help from God. You try to go it alone when you could really benefit from His help. You hesitate asking because you think God's got "bigger things to worry about" than my hangnail in life. When in reality, God often takes care of us through our friends.

Of course, Jesus modeled receiving. One particular story that comes to mind is the woman who washed Jesus' feet with her tears, wiped them with her hair, and then treated them to a bath of expensive perfume. (You can read the story in Luke 7:36–50.) Talk about receiving a sacrificial gift! And you and I have trouble letting someone do our dishes?

It's possible your family of origin instilled the lie of self-sufficiency in your head and heart. You watched mom and dad go it alone. Maybe they were short on compassion and big on telling you to "buck up" and figure it out. Looking back at the environment in which you grew up is not for the purpose of blaming. Instead it's valuable for understanding why we think the way we do. However, our thinking—our belief system—doesn't always tell us the truth. Sometimes we have to dig into it, see if it's being honest with us, and, if necessary, do some belief system remodeling to align our views about receiving with God's perspective.

This is important internal work for us to do because, as my friend Laura says, "There's incredible freedom found in realizing you don't have to carry the weight all on your own shoulders. Being freed from the pressure to handle it all, realizing you're really not alone, and understanding that people care and really do want to help is very liberating."

Pride, when it keeps us from asking for or accepting help, robs us of the community experience. It steals away the opportunity for someone to flex their serving muscles. It weakens the fibers of friendship. You and I have a responsibility to receive so others can give.

When I told Sue I was bringing dinner over, she immediately protested, "No, you don't need to do that. You're sick too!" I responded back, "No, Sue. You have no idea how much I NEED to do this." I'm grateful she received so I could experience the joy of giving.

THE GROWTH OF GIVING

Every story has two sides. The one we tell and the details we keep to ourselves. If I just told you the story of me making a quick decision to take Sue a meal, as I just did, it would be accurate but missing some details. You see, I actually struggled making that decision. After my initial burst of inspiration, I second-guessed myself with thoughts like, *It sure would be nice to have an extra meal in the freezer for a night when I don't feel well. Not only that, but things are tight financially. I shouldn't be giving food away when we're paying so many medical bills.* Without realizing it, I just about rationalized myself right out of serving. Thankfully, I pushed through the doubt and took the meal as God had prompted me to do.

Looking back, I can now see that my own fear and lack of trust kicked in. In this case, it was all about provision. Did I trust that God would provide for me and my family? Did I trust Him to provide meals for me when I needed them? Did I trust Him to provide financially for us even during this season of outrageous medical expenses? Could I surrender my fear to Him?

This kind of "pushing through" isn't lost on Jesus either. The night before His crucifixion, Jesus was in the garden of Gethsemane with His friends, the disciples. He knew the pain that was ahead of Him. The human side of Him did not want to experience that kind of pain. Pushing through those emotions, the Bible tells us that Jesus was in so much anguish that He was sweating blood (Luke 22:44 NIV). Jesus asks God, "Father, if you are willing, take this cup from me" (Luke 22:42a). He's putting His human desire on the table. He's telling God, "This is hard." He's saying, "If there's another plan in Your pocket, You can play that card now." Then He fully submits when He says, "Not my will, but yours be done" (Luke 22:42b).

In Mark 10:45 (NIV) we are reminded that Jesus "did not come to be served, but to serve, and to give his life as a ransom for many." Just like Jesus, we are designed to serve one another. In fact, I think there are three reasons why it's important for us to help others:

Serving matures us. When we give, it requires a sacrifice of time, energy, or resources that could have been used in another way. Sometimes we have to choose to do something for someone else when deep down we'd rather be doing something for ourselves. When we have to deny ourselves, we put our wants on the back burner and the needs of others on the front burner. Sacrifice brings about maturity. Therefore there is incredible growth in giving.

Serving allows us to use our talents. Sometimes when we serve, it's just plain old elbow grease. I mean, really, who has the spiritual gift of shoveling horse manure? The truth is we all do, when we deny ourselves and offer to help a friend who has a horse farm! Yet sometimes, we do get to offer something we're actually good at. Maybe home organization comes easy to you and you have a friend who is overwhelmed with her kitchen clutter. Your God-given this-is-easy talent can be such a gift to her!

Serving combats our natural bent toward self-centeredness. Philippians 2:3–4 (NIV) reminds us to "do nothing out of selfish ambition or vain conceit. Rather, in humility value others above yourselves, not looking to your own interests but each of you to the interests of the others." Looking out for our own interests is a natural, human response. Yet God's economy calls for us to be others-centered, not self-

We lived in the same neighborhood and became fast friends when we were both eight years old. I moved away a few years later and we stayed friends through the craziness of life! The very best thing about her is her godly wisdom; she's not a wife or a mother yet but because she's so deeply rooted in the Word of God, she gives His advice, not her own opinion or experience. On my journey as a wife and mother, she's been one of my best supporters as she reminds me what God has to say about whatever I'm dealing with in those areas. Our song is none other than Michael W. Smith's "Friends Are Friends Forever" song.—KRYSTAL

centered. God tells us, "No one should seek their own good, but the good of others" (1 Corinthians 10:24 NIV).

THAT'S EASY FOR ME! I LIKE TO HELP!

Words come easy to me. I've been known to proof a resume for a friend, or to help a friend write a cover letter for an application. My background in music has allowed me to serve as a consultant for friends on when to start piano lessons or whether to buy a keyboard or a piano. Now that I have walked through cancer, I'm able to help friends think about questions they should ask when they're on a difficult health journey. I enjoy clean eating and have learned a lot from both my daughters that I now pass along to friends who ask. I love helping friends in a pinch, and in this season of my life, if my schedule allows, I'm happy to help out at the last minute rather than planning weeks in advance.

I hate to shop. I particularly hate to shop for clothes. My friend Karrie has shopped for me for the last three years of what I wear onstage at Hearts at Home conferences. She has an eye for clothes and a love of shopping that I simply don't have. What a gift she gives me in making sure I have something flattering and comfortable to wear!

Too often we underestimate what we have to offer the world. We forget that things that come easy to us may be difficult for someone else. What do you do well? What comes easy to you? Do you garden? Do you have a specialty in the kitchen? Do you love kids? Enjoy being behind a camera? Maybe you have a way with words? Have a medical background that can offer wisdom in medical decisions? Do you have an innate ability to build something? Are you creative? A good problem solver? Crafty? Do you have an eye for decorating details? Make a mean crème brulee?

Are you good with money? Can you make people laugh? Love to shop? Enjoy organizing? Can pick out a dangling participle or misspelled word in something you read? Just enjoy helping, no matter what the job is?

God has made you with unique skills, talents, and interests. He's also allowed certain circumstances in your life that have given you unique experiences. One way God redeems the broken places in our lives is to allow us to bring empathy, wisdom, and encouragement to others who are walking a similar path. I love how 2 Corinthians 1:3–4 (NIV) confirms this, "Praise be to the God and Father of our Lord Jesus Christ, the Father of compassion and the God of all comfort, who comforts us in all our troubles, so that we can comfort those in any trouble with the comfort we ourselves receive from God."

He wants you to steward—or manage—those talents and experiences. Think outside the box on what comes easy to you. Consider what you enjoy that someone else might despise. Ponder the experiences you've had and the wisdom you've learned from those circumstances. Then contribute generously to the moms around you. We're truly better when we're supporting each other along the way.

I GOT YOU COVERED

While we were writing the book, Anne's husband was out of town for nearly three consecutive weeks. During his last nine-day trip, she tweeted, "So grateful to have a friend who takes my kids to the park with hers so I can have some downtime. 2 days down, 7 to go." It's moments like that where helping dovetails into caring. Turn the page and let's dig in to that!

FROM ANNE'S HEART

We have never had the luxury of living in the same community as family. As a new mom, I jumped at any offer that came my way from friends to watch my daughter. Seriously, as friends would say at church, "I'd love to babysit Rilyn so you guys could go on a date," I would say, "Great! When would be a good time?" I remember posting something on Facebook about saying yes to offers and an acquaintance said something to the effect of "Those offers will stop coming when you have more children." This made me so sad for my friends with multiple children, so I became much more intentional about asking my friends if they would benefit from me watching their children.

One friend in particular had three small children and I knew she was stretched thin. She often mentioned how she and her husband never had time together. On several occasions, I offered to watch her children and she always waved me off. I observed three possible reasons why my offer was rejected.

*1. **Lack of trust.** It's possible that she didn't trust me, personally, with her children. However, my gut feeling says this wasn't the case. I think it was more a lack of trust that anyone else could provide adequate care for her children. Here's the thing— no one will provide love and care like mom or dad. However, a child will not suffer from an hour or two away from parental care. In fact, it helps them learn to be independent and know that mom and dad will come back.*

2. **She didn't understand the value of time away from her children.** *One piece of wisdom from my mom that I hold near and dear to my heart is, "Taking care of yourself IS taking care of your family." Often we put ourselves onto the back burner to care for everyone else's needs. Yet, we are often left tired or emotionally empty. Errantly we tell ourselves, "This is a season. It's normal and I just have to push through." Yes we do need to do that sometimes, but we also need to be intentional about filling our own tanks.*

3. **She didn't know how to accept help.** *All too often, we fall into the trap of believing we burden others when they have the opportunity to serve us. Telling someone no when they offer help denies that person the opportunity to say yes when God prompts them to serve. This is what community is all about! It may feel uncomfortable at first, but start practicing saying yes! if help is ever offered.*

I received a text from Aimee one day asking if she could come to my house to stay with my children while I went to the store; I had mentioned to her in passing the day before that I hadn't been able to get to the grocery store with my newborn and two-year-old. At first, I was going to wave her off and thank her for the nice gesture, but I am so grateful that I instead answered yes. I got the opportunity to go to the store—alone!— and actually walk out with everything that was on my list! This is what "momming" together is all about!

SOMETHING TO THINK ABOUT:

*What fears have kept you from helping
or accepting help?*

Today's Friendship Assignment

Do you have a friend who's trying to get a project done? Offer to help her in some way!

Do you have a project you're trying to get finished? Ask a friend to help you!

Push through your fear and take a step toward creating or deepening a friendship.

CHAPTER 6

Caring Together
"You're not alone.
We're here for you."

To the amazing woman at Aldi's: You stopped what you were doing and helped me load my groceries even after I politely declined your help. You explained that you have five kids and when someone offers to help, let them. I am so grateful to you. You saw that I was overwhelmed and you were such a blessing! You had no knowledge of why I was so overwhelmed. My husband was out of town and I had gotten up and given my three kids a bath. I got us all ready for church, barely making it there on time. Filled my gas tank. Took all three kids— all who have special needs—to Walgreens fending off rapid-fire questions of why we can't get everything we lay our eyeballs on, went to JC Penney, and then took them grocery shopping. A trip that should have taken thirty minutes ended up taking an hour and a half. The kids were completely overstimulated, tired, and hungry by the time we were checking out. You heard the rude comment from the stranger about my kids. You told me to 'just ignore her and that people act like poops sometimes!' I don't know who you are but I DO know you were sent to me at just the right time! Your random act of kindness will not be forgotten!"

The above story was shared by my Facebook friend Michelle. She was so touched by this mom's kindness. It's a beautiful illustration of how to care for another mom . . . even one you don't know!

I love how Sandra Bullock described caring women in her life in a *People* magazine story "Bullock Cherishes Her 'Tribe,'" which includes close friends and family—and she especially cherishes the females. "If you are struggling, the women in my life descend like paratroopers en masse and will not leave your side until they know you are standing on your own two feet again," she explains. "No judgment, just support."[1]

From knowing our neighbors to caring for other moms in our tribe to reaching out in crisis, we need to know how to reach out to those around us. As we've already noted, taking care of others used to come naturally when people relied on friends and family for barn raisings, quilting circles, and everyday tasks we now have machines to do. Now many women don't know where to begin.

We've established that we're better together. We understand the responsibility of receiving and the gift of giving. We're pushing through our fear. Now let's sharpen our skills for practically caring for one another.

CARING EVERY DAY

Stephanie said this about a friend of hers: "During a time of depression, she called me every day. She shared Scripture, helped with my babies, prepared meals, helped me clean my house, and prayed for me. She didn't ask, she did."

I love that—"She didn't ask, she did." That's how we help one another; we *do*. What exactly do we "do"? There are eight gifts you and I can give another mom on a regular basis.

The Gift of Thoughtfulness

Terri says that after she quit her job, it meant the world to her when a former coworker sent her occasional texts letting her know she was thinking of her. Doing that for someone who moves, or changes churches, or no longer volunteers at school shows that you care for them beyond the relationship of convenience that originally brought you together.

My friend Laura says, "Rare indeed is the mom friend who goes to the effort to stay in touch when it becomes less convenient. Moms are busy; it's understandable that we are more likely to stay in contact with the people we see most frequently. However, sometimes when there's been a change of some sort and they're no longer as involved, that is the exact time someone needs to most be remembered. Plus, it communicates the powerful message of valuing someone as a person even if they are no longer 'doing' whatever it was that brought you together in the first place—volunteering at school, attending the same church, ministry project within the church, etc." Can you think of someone you've not seen in a while? What if you sent her a text, a note, or connected with her through social media just to let her know that God brought her to your mind? The gift of thoughtfulness is so powerful!

When Lynda's five-month-old son passed away, her neighbor would leave an encouraging note and a white rose on her porch on the ninth of each month. "It was beautiful that she just left it for me to find so that I could have a private quiet moment in honor of my baby. Yet by her remembering the flower each month, it let me know she remembered David, she cared, and she was there if I needed to talk, get a hug, or have someone to cry with."

Bethany recalls, "I had a miscarriage with our first baby in January. That year on Mother's Day I received a card and Precious Moments figurine (I collect them) that said, 'A mom's love is the best gift of all' from my college friend Sarah. This really blessed me and I have thought of it often through the years. It showed me just how much it means for someone to remember you during times of sadness and pain."

When life is hard or a loss is experienced, something as simple as a text that says, "I'm thinking of you," can make all the difference in the world. If you have a friend who experiences a loss, use an electronic calendar (online or on a smartphone) to create a recurring event on the date of their loss. That date will forever be etched in their mind and heart. You remembering the date will rank as one of the most thoughtful gifts they've ever received.

The Gift of Sensitivity

My friend Olivia's best friend had been facing infertility, and here was Olivia pregnant . . . again. Having gone through infertility herself, she knew pregnancy news was *never* easy to hear. After praying about it, Olivia decided to tell her friend on their weekly walk. That way, she wouldn't have to make a lot of eye contact immediately, but she *would* be thankful to hear that news in person. For another friend, though, Olivia decided a heartfelt letter was a better option—providing that friend privacy and space.

There's no perfect way to break the news of a baby on the way to a friend going through infertility. It'll probably sting. But being sensitive, loving, and honest in sharing sooner rather than later will go a long way. Too often life moves along so fast, we unintentionally overlook thinking of others. Giving a friend the gift of sensitivity can really honor a friendship.

The Gift of Presence

When my husband, Mark, went through a deep depression and left for three months, three of my friends were at my house within an hour. One brought a suitcase and stayed for three days. There was nothing they could "do" to make it better, but they were determined that I wouldn't go through it alone. Their gift of presence was a beautiful gift to me.

My friend Lisa tells about one of her friends who sat through eight chemo treatments with her, four of those treatments lasting eight hours each. Another friend, Laura, who was also facing cancer, said her best friend went with her to her first oncologist appointment.

Heather says, "When I lost my son Seth, my friend drove three hours to be with my kids so my husband and I could plan his celebration of life service. When I got home, she was playing board games with them, and

I met a dear sister when living as an American expat in London. We met when we were both pregnant with our first child and ended up each having three children very close in age. We've both moved many times yet we get together on the phone or visit at least once a year. Distance doesn't keep us apart! Our kids teethed together, and then we visited sick dads in the hospital together. Now that we are nearly empty nesters we're planning to get together more often. We have walked hand in hand and heart to heart for twenty-two years— even living across the country.—CHRISTINE

afterward came over and held my hand as all I could do in that moment was cry. No words were said but prayers were definitely felt. It was comforting to know that my children were being loved on and cared for when I couldn't even hold my head up."

Nobody should go through life alone. Take notice of the women around you. Pay attention to ways you can let them know you care on a regular basis.

The Gift of Physical Help

My friend Becky offers this gift on a regular basis. She comes over and just says, "What do you have that needs to be done? Let's get it done!" It could be laundry, changing bedsheets, organizing something, cleaning, weeding the garden—anything! Her help has been a game-changer for me so many times. While she's been there for me in times of crisis, she often offers this gift during everyday life. She'll say, "Let's get a date on the calendar and I'll help you do whatever is bugging you the most!"

Robin shared with me about the physical gift of help friends gave her when her mother was in hospice. Many meals were delivered, and she had one friend take her for a car ride just to get out of the house for a few minutes while her mom was on hospice care in her home. After her mom passed away, a friend got a house key from another friend and cleaned her house while she was out of town arranging the memorial service. Another friend was at the house when the company that provided the bed, oxygen, and other hospice supplies came to the house to pick it all up. This spared her the pain of being there.

Lisa tells of a friend who came over and made her lunch when she was recovering from being in the hospital. Physical help doesn't always have to be something we do ourselves . . . it can also be a service we provide. During my cancer journey, we received several restaurant gift cards that provided meals on nights I just couldn't cook. Molly had hip surgery and was under "no weight bearing" orders for four weeks. A fantastic friend sent a cleaning company over to clean every two weeks during her recovery period. Brooke's friend helped her financially so she could see her dying mother on what would be her last Mother's Day.

Don't ask . . . just do!

The Gift of Spiritual Help

When I was going through my cancer treatment, I had a friend who texted me every week with a Scripture of encouragement. I passed on that same encouragement to another friend who was a few months behind me in cancer treatment. Kory says her friend "loves me where I am and points me to Christ." Kitty says, "My friend led me to Bible study at a time when I desperately needed to go." Crystal says, "I so appreciate my friend speaking truth to me in love." Karen treasures a time when a friend prayed with and for her during a hard parenting season.

When the mountains of life get big, having someone to help you keep your eyes on the Mountain Mover can make all the difference in the world. Here are some Scriptures you can share with a friend who is going through a hard time:

Proverbs 3:5–6—Trust in the LORD with all your heart, and do not lean on your own understanding. In all your ways acknowledge him, and he will make straight your paths.

Psalm 34:18—The LORD is near to the brokenhearted and saves the crushed in spirit.

James 1:12—Blessed is the one who perseveres under trial because, having stood the test, that person will receive the crown of life that the Lord has promised to those who love him.

Psalm 46:1—God is our refuge and strength, an ever-present help in trouble.

Isaiah 41:10—So do not fear, for I am with you; do not be dismayed, for I am your God. I will strengthen you and help you; I will uphold you with my righteous right hand.

Philippians 4:6—Do not worry about anything, but in everything by prayer and supplication with thanksgiving let your requests be made known to God. And the peace of God, which surpasses all understanding, will guard your hearts and your minds in Christ Jesus.

(If you'd like more Bible verses that bring encouragement during tough times, you'll find thirty-three more verses in appendix D.)

The Gift of Listening

Sometimes just having someone to listen can make all the difference in the world. Most women long to be heard more than to have their problems fixed. When we can be a safe person for a friend to be real and raw without judgment, we give them an incredible gift.

Amber recalls when a girlfriend walked with her through the months following the suicide of her best friend since childhood: "She supported me while I grieved and came to terms with everything." Robin says, "Knowing I can be honest and sort through my feelings without being judged makes such a difference."

Here are four steps to becoming a better listener:

1) *Stop.* Stop what you're doing and give your friend your full attention. Maintain eye contact as much as possible. If you're talking on the phone, move to a room where there are no distractions, if possible.

2) *Empathize.* Put yourself in your friend's shoes. Respond with statements like, "That must have been so painful," or "I'm so sorry," or "That breaks my heart. I can see how it has broken your heart." As your friend is talking, you can nod, or say small, soft words, like "Oh," or "Uh huh," or even "Keep talking," to let her know you are hearing her. Resist the urge to move the attention to yourself; just listen without looking for ways to interject your thoughts.

3) *Comfort.* Give a hug. Let her cry. Don't feel like you have to fix anything.

4) *Follow up.* If your friend is going through something hard, check back in with a text or a phone call to see how she's doing. Don't hesitate to write down the name of any other people she mentions when she's talking. This will help you follow up by name. (I write this kind of information in a little prayer notebook I keep.)

The Gift of Stepping In

Lisa shares, "The week after my dad died, I took my kids to the park. My friend called and asked if she and her kids could meet us there. She showed up and said, 'I'll take it from here. Go home, take a nap, and have a quiet dinner.' She took my kids back to her house for the rest of the day, fed them dinner, and brought them home at bedtime. She knew just how to help the friend who never asks for help."

When my friend Jill's father died, she recalled, "Two friends came to my house and prepared dinner for all the family and some extended family while we were at the visitation. To come home to those sweet faces and the meal they had ready for us spoke volumes of the love they have for me and my family."

When we say, "Just let me know what you need," we're putting the burden of responsibility on the person needing help.

Rachel recalls, "My husband was out of the country when I miscarried our baby. My closest friend took me to the hospital and stayed with me. Another dear friend brought me white crocheted baby booties to give me something tangible to touch. Another loved through a very practical gift by bringing me feminine hygiene products. Powerful love demonstrated three different ways."

Gail says, "When my husband left me and our two young children, I had to continue to work but also had to move out of our house to something less expensive. Without me asking or saying a word, my friend and her twelve-year-old daughter went to my house and packed all day every day for a week (while I was at work) and hauled the boxes to storage or to the apartment where we were moving."

I love these stories, because they illustrate the many ways "she didn't ask, she did" can be lived out. In each story there was a giver and a receiver and both benefit because helping others is helping yourself. When He lived on this earth, Jesus talked, touched, visited, helped, and even laughed with those He loved. He responded in crisis, He cried, and He gave love and grace in everyday life. We get the opportunity to follow in His footsteps when there are needs around us. Having been on the receiving end of the care of others, I have found that the more specific the offer, the better it is for the receiver. When someone is in crisis or just overwhelmed with everyday mom life, they often don't have the mental or emotional capacity to remember who to call when they realize they do need help with something. When we say, "Just let me know what you need," we're putting the burden of responsibility on the person needing help. If life is hard or they're in crisis, they don't need one more decision to make! Do you know someone who is in crisis, lonely, grieving, recovering, or even just had a baby? Rather than saying, "Let me know if you need anything," try one of these offers:

- I have next Thursday available; can I take your kids for a few hours?

- I'd like to come clean your house for you; can I come do that on Tuesday?

- I'd like to bring you dinner; will tomorrow night work?

- I have two hours on Tuesday evening free. What needs to be done that is bugging you that I can do for you?

- I'm headed to the store. Is there anything I can pick up for you?

- I'm running some errands this afternoon. Can I drop by for a thirty-minute visit?

- Here's a gift card and delivery menu—dinner's on us tonight.

My friend Becky offered to come over and help me the day before my lumpectomy surgery. She said, "I'm here to help you get done whatever you really want to get done before you're down for a while." She helped me do a little cooking, cleaning, and organizing. She also helped me get the guest room ready for my mom to arrive. We laughed later that I was "surgery nesting" because I was a cleaning/reorganizing machine that day.

Two days after my surgery, my friend Lisa asked me if she could come over and wrap my Christmas presents. She and her teenage daughter came over and wrapped gifts while I recovered from surgery and Mark was at work. What a gift that was for me and for Mark because the whole job would have fallen to him since I only had use of one arm!

Both of these friends and others like them have been Jesus with skin on! Their offers were specific and easier to say yes to than a generic offer. They blessed both me and my family. We're all in the ministry of availability—some of us just may not know it. God will use you to help, encourage, and care for others if you'll keep your eyes open to see the need and your heart available to care for others. Sometimes, however, crisis hits and you may need to step in to run triage for a friend.

CARING IN A CRISIS

My friend Cheri Keaggy released a powerful album three years ago. "So I Can Tell" is the light that has come out of a dark season of Cheri's life. The songs are heartfelt expressions of a woman who has come to know God deeply through pain. Cheri sent one my way three years ago when my marriage went through its darkest season.

When I got to the third song on the album, the tears started flowing. The song was titled "When You Were Jesus to Me." Until the night that Mark left, I had never experienced anything close to an emotional crisis. I was so crushed by grief that it was squeezing the life out of me. Even cancer wasn't as hard as the emotional pain I experienced in that season of my marriage.

As I walked through that dark season, God greatly increased my empathy, compassion, and mercy. More than that, through the loving actions of my dearest friends, He also showed me how to respond in a crisis. My friends were truly Jesus to me.

You may not need this now—but at some point, it's likely you'll have the opportunity to "be Jesus with skin on" to a friend in crisis. Here are some tangible ways to make a difference when a friend faces the unthinkable:

When in crisis, sometimes there are no words to utter to God . . . just tears.

1) **Be there.** Stay with her. Don't feel like you need to say any words, just hold her and let her weep. This is the gift of presence taken to a critical level. My friend Becky did this for me. She was at my house within the hour and she didn't leave until two days later. I'm grateful even three years later to Becky's husband, Dave, who supported her staying with me for that long. Eventually my sister came for a couple of days and then my dad came and stayed for four more days. This support was so important for me and for my teenage boys who were still at home.

One night when Becky was there, she heard me crying in bed in the middle of the night. She sneaked in my bedroom, crawled in bed with me, and held me while I cried. No words were spoken, only comfort was given. Heather, who lost her nearly two-year-old son, said that her friends who were good listeners were the best gift for her. She said, "it isn't what you say but rather what you pray" that makes a difference. "Just them recognizing the hurt, sorrow, pain, and anguish that is a part of our journey of walking through grief is comforting," she shared.

2) **Think *for* the person.** When crisis hits, the last thing that person can do is think about taking care of themselves. In those first few days, I honestly don't think I would have had anything to eat or drink if Becky or my sister Juli had not actually put the plate of food or the glass of water in front of me and said, "Eat" or "Drink." When someone is in crisis, they need a friend or family member who will take over the logical thinking those first days and weeks. You might even run interference for them by serving as the coordinator of meals or starting a private Facebook page for friends and family to get updates and information.

3) **Provide food**. My friends Crystal and Lisa, who also stayed with me until well after midnight the first night, brought meals throughout that first weekend. Eventually my Hearts at Home family and church family set up a meal plan for several weeks. This was so helpful because I suddenly had so many other things I had to tend to. My friend Tina, who lost her husband after just a few years of marriage, says that those meals brought in the early weeks after his death were literally life-sustaining for her daughter and her. Tip: When you take a friend a meal, take it in disposable containers so the recipient doesn't have to worry about returning anything to you. You might even bring some premade peanut butter and jelly sandwiches cut into triangles for a weary mom to have on hand to feed her always-hungry kids.

4) **Help with daily routine stuff.** Becky, Crystal, and Juli cleaned, did dishes, made guest beds, ran to the store, picked up prescriptions . . . you name it . . . they did it. I was so thankful. For the first month, my friend

Crystal called me anytime she was running to the store to see if I needed anything. I was so thankful because this kept me out of public settings where I could emotionally lose it so easily.

5) **Do any "unpleasant" tasks.** When Mark requested more of his personal belongings, I could not emotionally handle packing those things up. Crystal and Becky did that job for me. If the crisis involves a death, this can particularly be helpful when that friend is ready to part with the personal belongings of the person who has died. Even answering phone calls can be an "unpleasant" task. Don't hesitate to do that for the person to protect them from having to share the story one more time.

6) **Don't be afraid to help.** If you are a close friend or you seem to be the only person reaching out, you are not infringing on their privacy . . . you are helping them survive. I always worried about infringing on someone's privacy in times of crisis until I was on the receiving side of crisis. I had trouble functioning, especially in the early days. I was so thankful for friends and family who filled my gaps.

7) **Pray with and for the person.** When in crisis, sometimes there are no words to utter to God . . . just tears. Sometimes you can just be there, and sometimes you can be the one to utter the words to God on their behalf. Heather says after her son's death, "For months my closest friends sent text messages all throughout the night, as they knew I wasn't sleeping. They prayed circles of protection around our home."

We all need each other. In good times and bad, we're designed to live in community with other people. More than anything, when we care for one another, we're Jesus with skin on. No friend will ever forget a time when you were Jesus to her.

Caring for others allows us to more easily share with others because we know that we all go through hard times. Taking off our masks is an important part of taking friendship to a deeper level. Turn the page and let's talk turkey about sharing tough times.

FROM ANNE'S HEART

"I am so glad you don't have children," Bekki said to me with a sigh of relief across the coffee-shop table. I was nowhere near having children at this time of my life, but all of our friends seemed to be starting off their families. I had called Bekki to ask if she wanted to grab some coffee together. At the time, I laughed at the absurdity of her relief, but now as a mother myself, I completely understand where she was coming from. Personally, I need time away from being "mom" and conversations about children and parenting.

As I consider my mothering tribe, it is quite a patchwork of people. There are three women in particular who have been kindred spirits—and none of them have children. Rachel and I were friends before I had children. And while it has been difficult navigating the changing seasons, we still get each other. She knew me better than anyone else. I was able to be myself with her.

Kristen, Jill, and I connected instantly. We just clicked. We understood one another. The fact that we have different family structures has never hindered our ability to laugh together, cry on each other's shoulders, or encourage one another. While none of us truly understands the season the other is in, we are still able to listen and encourage. Their friendship also allows me an opportunity to explore all of the facets of the woman God created me to be—not just mom.

There are a few principles I've learned or am trying to master in navigating friendships with a non-mom:

1. **It takes effort on your part.** *Sometimes, it's much easier to forge friendships with other moms because you can bring the kids along on a playdate or they can empathize with your parenting wins or frustrations. While non-moms may enjoy occasional time with your children, their friendship is more than that. Find time to meet without children. Ask her questions about herself.*

2. **Don't dominate the conversation with stories of motherhood.** *While non-mom friends can certainly sympathize with your "parenting-a-four-year-old struggles," it's important to engage all the other facets of life in your conversation. Having a hard time thinking of non-kid things to talk about? Check out the "Questions in a Box" app. It is a great tool to use as a springboard for conversation.*

3. **They may occasionally enjoy babysitting for you—but don't overuse their generosity.** *When Rilyn was an infant, Rachel was a natural choice for a babysitter. I fully trusted her and she tended to have a more flexible schedule. At one point, I realized that lately I had only seen her when she came to*

babysit Rilyn—which had been quite a bit. I decided to pull that back in balance. Intentionally keeping the friendship as a priority is important.

SOMETHING TO THINK ABOUT:
Have you considered pursuing friendship with someone who doesn't have kids?

Today's Friendship Assignment

Who needs to know you care?

Who needs you to be Jesus with skin on?

Who can you be a blessing to this week?

CHAPTER 7

Sharing Together
"Really? You feel that
way too?"

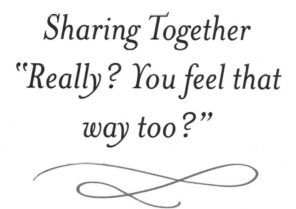

I received a call from a ministry friend who was desperate. She needed to talk to someone and God kept prompting her heart to talk to me so we set up a time to talk. We sat on my front porch in cozy chairs, sipping tea. Using probably half a box of Kleenex, she poured out her story. She had recently discovered her husband had been having an emotional affair through Facebook with an old high school girlfriend. She was mortified, devastated, sick to her stomach, embarrassed, and completely lost on what to do. She had kept it to herself for weeks but the hurt and confusion were so deep she needed to process this with someone. That's when she started praying about who to talk to, and God kept telling her it was me. She couldn't imagine why I would be good to talk to, but she decided to be obedient and made the call.

What she didn't know is the exact same situation had happened to me two years earlier, but my husband's emotional affair had eventually become a physical affair. However, Mark and I had not yet shared about that part of our story publicly. We were still healing and only those in our inside circle knew all that had happened.

I listened to her story and before she wallowed in her pain and shame any longer, I said, "I understand all too well. That was our story, but unfortunately ours included crossing into the physical. You are not alone." She sat there with tears streaming down her face, nearly stopped in her tracks, and said, "I had no idea. I am so sorry. Oh my goodness, you really do understand what I'm feeling, don't you?"

Earlier we stated that the most powerful four words a mom can hear are YOU ARE NOT ALONE. When I shared those words with my friend that day, a huge weight was lifted off her shoulders. The shame began to dissipate. The relief was nearly tangible.

We talked regularly over the next few months as she navigated emotions, boundaries, and communication with her husband. Many times the conversations would start with, "This is what I'm feeling . . . is that normal?" Every feeling, every emotion, every struggle she had was something I'd experienced in some way. My ability to share my story helped her walk through her story. My ability to pray for her specifically gave her the spiritual support she desperately needed.

When we share our stories with others, we live out 2 Corinthians 1: 3–4, "[God] comes alongside us when we go through hard times, and before you know it, he brings us alongside someone else who is going through hard times so that we can be there for that person just as God was there for us" (THE MESSAGE). Sharing your story helps another mom walk through her story. My friend Suzie Eller says, "As you mend, you move from needing help to giving help."

Of course, you don't have to share your story as I have on my blog, on a stage, or in a book. You just need to steward your story when God gives you the opportunity to share. Each of us has a story that can encourage others. Each of us can give "a reason for the hope that is in you" (1 Peter 3:15).

WHAT'S YOUR STORY?

One of the "getting to know you" questions I often ask when I'm visiting with someone I don't know well is, "So, what's your story?" It's a broad question, but I've never had anyone not understand what I'm asking. Sometimes they'll clarify, "Do you mean my faith story or my life story?" I tell them either one is fine with me. Usually they'll laugh, look at their watch, and say, "Well, how long do you have?" I encourage them to simply give me their highlights.

Have you ever shared your story in a short, succinct, give-someone-the-highlights kind of way? This isn't where you share your darkest secrets. It's where you give them a bird's-eye view of the journey that has brought you to today. Anne and I will share ours with you to give you an example of what we're talking about.

My story: I grew up in Avon, Indiana, which is a western suburb of Indianapolis, Indiana. My dad was an English teacher/principal/superintendent. My mom was a stay-at-home mom until my two sisters and I were in school and then she got a job as a school secretary. I grew up attending the United Methodist Church with my family. After high school, I attended Butler University, majoring in choral music education. I met my hubby on a blind date right before I started at Butler. We got married after my freshman year of college, had Anne, our first child, during my junior year and Evan, our second, on my college graduation day. Needless to say, Butler mailed me my diploma. Mark worked for a family business when we married but felt called to ministry so we packed up our little family and moved to Lincoln, Illinois, so he could attend Lincoln Bible College. I was a day-care provider by day and worked in a dinner theatre by night to make ends meet. When Mark was offered an internship at a large church in Bloomington, Illinois, we moved our family and he commuted to school. I taught piano and voice lessons for fifteen years until our youngest was born. By that time, Hearts at Home, the ministry to moms I started, was growing faster than I ever imagined and we had adopted a son from Russia, bringing us to a grand total of five kids. Mark was a pastor for twenty years and now owns his own home remodeling business. Our kids are grown, ranging in age from nineteen to thirty-one. We just celebrated our thirty-second wedding anniversary (which has been hard-earned!), and we have three grandkids who call us Nana and Papaw.

My friend Michelle and I met on our sons' first day of kindergarten. It was the first year the school was going to full-day kindergarten after having a half-day program. They gave parents the option of picking up kids at noon if they wanted to have them only go half day. Out of seventy families, she and I were the only ones there picking up our kids early. We enjoyed our sons' company and weren't ready to send them off for a full day. We've been friends ever since!—CARRIE

Do you see how hearing my story gave you some connecting points you might not have known? If we'd been sitting down having a cup of tea together, it likely would have prompted some questions that could have led to great conversation. Here's Anne's story:

"I grew up in Bloomington-Normal, Illinois. I'm the oldest of five kids, four biological and one adopted. My dad was a pastor of a non-denominational church and now owns his own home remodeling business. My mom was a stay-at-home mom who eventually started Hearts at Home, a ministry for moms. She now leads Hearts at Home and speaks and writes. After I graduated from high school, I attended Taylor University for a year and a half and then Illinois State University for a semester. I met my husband at Starbucks (of all places!) while attending ISU. We dated for several months and then I left to become a nanny for four months in Paris, France. Without me knowing, he arranged to come to Paris, had my friends get me up on the Eiffel Tower under false pretenses, surprised me, and asked me to marry him. I returned home to work for nine months and plan a wedding. My husband, Matt, is a youth pastor. For the first seven years of our marriage, we served a church in Zion, Illinois. Rilyn came along after we'd been married five years. Landon followed two years later. They are five and three now. Almost two years ago, we moved to Springfield, Illinois, where Matt is a family life pastor and I run a day care in my home."

So what about you? Take a few minutes and think about your story. Either in your head or out loud, form a two- to three-minute version that gives the highlights of your journey. Think about the pieces of your story that may connect with another mom in some way: where you grew up, any post–high school schooling, what you did BK (before kids), adoptive or biological journey, and stage of life now. Hearing someone's story or sharing your story is somewhat like peeking through the window of a house you might want to enter. Similar to the "getting to know you questions" you use in a TBF situation, it lets you come to understand what experiences have formed and shaped someone.

TBF—TRYING TO BE FRIENDS
MBF—MIGHT BE FRIENDS
GGF—GOOD GIRLFRIEND
BFF—BEST FRIEND FOREVER

You can also share your faith story. As an example, here's mine: I grew up attending church. My family's commitment to church gave me a great foundation of faith. However, as I entered college, I longed for something more. It was a sorority sister who helped me move from religion to relationship. She introduced me to a personal relationship with Jesus Christ. When I met my husband, Mark, he was a new believer who had accepted Christ at a Billy Graham Crusade. We've both grown in our faith together throughout our marriage. When I think about my own personal spiritual influences, I'd have to say my Mom-2Mom moms group, over twenty years of Hearts at Home conferences, being a part of a Moms In Prayer group, digging into God's Word for wisdom, having some strong Christian friends, and being in good churches have been essential pieces of growing my faith.

Here's Anne's: "Faith has always been a part of my life. I grew up in the church but also with parents who showed me how to live out faith on a daily basis. When I was eight years old, I accepted Christ and was baptized. However, I would say that I really moved from my parents' faith to my own faith in high school. This is when I had to make the decision of who I was going to be when my parents weren't looking. Would I follow Jesus or the world? I ultimately discovered life with Jesus was way better.

I am grateful for the foundation my parents set for me and hope to do the same for my children."

We have our life story, our faith story, and then we have the experience stories. These are life circumstances we've walked through and how God has grown us through those experiences. My experience stories include living on very little money when Mark was in school, doing day care in my home, adopting a child from Russia, having a prodigal child who doesn't share our family's faith, surviving breast cancer, mending our marriage after infidelity, and having a son with multiple mental health diagnoses. These are the stories I carry with me, asking God daily how He wants me to leverage them for His good. My marriage experience story is the one I shared with my desperate friend that day she needed to hear it.

You have these stories too. Maybe you've never thought of them as stories, but they are. In fact, they are your backstories. The ones you carry in your heart but people don't necessarily know about unless you tell them. Some of the life circumstances you've experienced are positive stories that illustrate hope, courage,

> *Your outside appearance doesn't usually communicate the circumstances that have shaped you.*

and faith. Some of the life circumstances you've experienced are painful stories that exemplify redemption, recovery, and restoration. These are sometimes the hardest stories to share but walking through them ultimately gives us more depth and the potential to be a better friend. Your outside appearance usually doesn't communicate the circumstances that have shaped you.

This is why we have to be careful about comparing ourselves to other moms. We can only see what they let us see. Because I've battled the "Perfection Infection" in my own life, I know how hard it is to take off that mask. I shared in my *No More Perfect Moms* book that the Perfection Infection happens when we unfairly compare ourselves to others, resulting in unrealistic expectations of ourselves and others. One of the strategies I've learned to keep the Perfection Infection at bay is when I'm tempted to compare myself to another mom, I say to myself, "She has a backstory that I don't know." That little reminder pulls me back from the ledge of comparison and plants me on the firm foundation of reality.

We have to be careful about comparing ourselves to other moms. We can only see what they let us see.

So if we all have a story and we're supposed to let God use our story, how do we get over the fear of putting our stuff out there? How can we find the courage to take off our masks and share honestly when God taps us on the shoulder and says, "Now please?"

I'm glad you asked! It all comes down to where we get our value.

YOUR STORY DOESN'T DEFINE YOU

Our world tries hard to define us in so many different ways: the cars we drive, the houses or neighborhoods where we live, our kids' behavior (good and bad), our appearance, college degrees, job titles, our husband's job, salary, and the list goes on and on. These counterfeit value determinants are a moving target in our ever-changing world. We fight these bogus beliefs nearly every day, but then we add in our own stories to falsely further determine value. Stories of success seem to add value to our lives. Stories of perceived failure seem to subtract value from our lives. It's as if we're on a never-ending teeter-totter ride that throws us up and down from one circumstance of life to another.

So what exactly determines value? In the art world there are two people that determine the value of art: the creator and the purchaser. Regardless of whether it's a painting, a photograph, a drawing, or a sculpture, the creator puts her whole self into the creation. Then she sets a value—or price—on the work. Along comes the purchaser. He sees the artwork and determines how much he will pay for the design. When a piece of art is eventually purchased, the value is determined by the price set by the creator and the price paid by the purchaser.

It's no different with our value. In the early pages of the book of Genesis, we read about God creating the heavens and the earth and everything on the earth. He made man and woman and put them in charge of every living thing (Genesis 1:28). Later in the book of Psalms, we are reminded that God intricately designed each one of us when He "knit you together in your mother's womb" (Psalm 139:13). Our Creator determined our value from the moment of creation and conception.

However, our broken world resulted in a broken relationship with God, going all the way back to Adam and Eve in the garden and their issue with eating fruit they weren't supposed to touch. But God's plan wasn't finished. God sent His Son, Jesus, to earth. He came as a baby, lived thirty-three years as fully God and fully man, then died a horrific death on the cross for us. In His death, Jesus closed the gap between a holy God and His unholy people. Jesus purchased God's creation with His life! That is the ultimate value statement, and the best part is that it never changes! No up-and-down teeter-totter value. No circumstances making us "more than" or "less than." Our life may be the sum of our experiences, but our value is determined by the totality of our God.

Our stories—good and bad—do not define us. Our God—always good—defines us. It's this truth that allows us to remove our masks. It's this truth that let's us assure another mom she's not alone. It's this truth that frees us to steward our story for God's purposes.

Even if your story is about a poor choice you or someone else made. Even if your story doesn't represent you or your family well. Even if it's a part of your life you'd rather forget. God can use your heartache to heal someone else's. He's adept at turning ashes into beauty (Isaiah 61:3). Heartache into help. Sorrow into joy. Don't underestimate what you have to offer. To the world, you may be just one woman. But to another woman who needs to hear your story, you may be the world.

LIMIT OR LAUNCH?

Your stories play a powerful role in your life. They are either the source of your shame or the spark in your game. You are the one who decides if your past will limit or launch you.

If you feel defined by your story, it will likely hold you back. Satan, the enemy of your soul, will use it to fuel condemnation. Condemnation hollows out your heart with blame and shame. Then blame and shame join forces to keep the story hidden away. Or so we think.

In reality, when we limit our stories and we believe they are tucked away for safekeeping, they often leak out—in control, anger, fear, insecurity, passivity, or mistrust. They can also leak out in emotional eating, addictions, and a lack of vulnerability in relationships.

I'm not suggesting by any means that you go out and shout your deepest, darkest secrets from the mountaintop. What I am asking you to consider is—if your story still brings about deep shame or the pain of condemnation, it most likely is affecting your life and relationships in some way. Processing it with a counselor, a pastor, or a good friend who can ask questions and help you think through how this has affected your life and could still be affecting your relationships in ways you've never considered is an important step toward healing. The enemy is an expert at whispering lies to us in times of pain, loss, and disappointment. When we can identify the lies and replace them with truth, we experience the freedom we're longing for.

Here are some real-life examples of moms I've had the privilege of helping with this process (names have been changed). Tina lost a child in a home accident. The shame she carried for many years limited her ability to help others and leaked into her relationships in ways she hadn't seen. Deep inside she blamed herself for the accident so she could never share it with anyone else because the shame moved it from "a bad accident" to "I'm a bad person because the accident happened." When Tina unpacked all the emotions she felt and the lies she believed, she started to see this was fueling her need to control every aspect of her family's life. While she felt like she was simply "running a tight ship," her need to control was suffocating her relationships with her husband and kids. She also discovered that deep down she believed she was a failure because the accident happened on her watch. This led her to the lie that she wasn't "worthy" of having a friend (who wants a friend who's a failure?). After sorting through it with her pastor, today Tina partners with her church behind-the-scenes whenever a family experiences the death of a child.

She offers wisdom to the pastors on how to best minister to the family and reaches out to the mom as a friend who truly understands.

Julie was a sexual abuse survivor, abused by her stepfather for many years. She had received counseling as a teen, in the months after the abuse was uncovered. However, as an adult, her experience was unknowingly leaking into her life and relationships. Julie's addiction to food kept her "unattractive" to men, reducing the fear of being abused once again but keeping her physically unhealthy. Learning to keep the abuse a secret planted the lie that you can't share anything with anyone. While she "knew" that wasn't true, she still felt it and believed it. She longed for deeper friendships, but seemed unable to move them past the surface level. In desperation, Julie found enough courage to reach out to her moms-group leader who listened carefully as she told her story. She encouraged Julie to talk to a Christian counselor who, over a matter of months, helped her sort through her past and how it was affecting her today. Julie moved from being limited by her story into wanting to launch it for God's purposes. She decided to share her story at her moms group. Her willingness to share her story helped two other moms begin to deal with their own abuse stories.

Exchanging your shame for God's grace will free you to be defined by your Creator rather than your circumstances. It will also launch you into a freedom to leverage it for God's good, when needed. While your struggles are very personal, they are not unique. The same feelings of discouragement, hopelessness, loss, shame, despair, depression, and grief are experienced by moms all over the world. Even if it's only one mom who hears your story, she can find strength, hope, and healing for her story.

Where do we share our story?

In the early years of our Hearts at Home conferences, we started something called "My Story." This is where we invite two or three moms to share their experience stories. Moms have shared stories of miscarriages, surviving infidelity, moving from two incomes to one income, becoming a widow, giving a child up for adoption, coming to know Jesus, blended family adjustment, parenting a special needs child, dealing with depression, parenting a prodigal child, and more. Women's lives have been just as deeply touched by these stories shared by everyday moms as they have from the keynote speaker's message. However, you don't have to stand on a stage in front of thousands of women to share your story.

These days you can connect with another hurting mom through social media. I've connected with many women through Facebook who are walking through breast cancer. Sometimes I see their posts and reach out to them. Some have taken me up on the offer of conversation through Facebook, others have not. Sometimes a friend can connect the dots between you and someone who needs to hear your story. Some people choose to write about their story on a blog;

They always say a best friend is someone you can call in the middle of the night when you need her. I met my best friend in first grade, and we have remained so close for fifteen years. I had to call her and her husband at 12:15 a.m. on Christmas Day as they were leaving Midnight Mass to come stay all night with my son while we prayed for a miracle at our daughter Brenna's bedside in 2011. She stayed up all night, texting and praying for us. I will never forget her loyalty and willingness to drop everything on Christmas for me!
—COURTNEY

some do so anonymously. When I learned about my husband's affair, I scanned the Internet for information on recovering from an affair. I found one woman's blog that really gave me the hope and encouragement I needed in that dark hour. The blog was written anonymously, so I will probably never meet the person who wrote those words, but her willingness to share her story gave me hope for my story.

Do make a commitment to honor your loved one when you speak about your story that's also their story.

Sitting in your kitchen sharing a cup of coffee and chatting with another mom is where many stories are shared. Or in the foyer after church. Or in an email. Or at a moms group. Or in a handwritten note. Or in a Bible study. Or in a small group. Or with a mentor. Or wherever God taps you on the shoulder and whispers, "This would be a good time for you to let her know she's not alone." Bottom line: Your story is so powerful when it's shared and God gets the high five!

FAQS ON SHARING

What if my story is also someone else's story? Our lives are intertwined so our stories tend to intermingle. What do you do about sharing your story when it's also your spouse's story? Or your son's or daughter's story? Or your stepfather's story? In some cases you're able to share your story without sharing specific details or even identifying others who were involved. Yet other times you may not be able to do that.

Certainly if you're going to share your story publicly, you'll want to agree upon what details you're both comfortable with being shared. When I share my family's stories when I'm speaking or writing a book or a blog post, I have a conversation with the person to determine if they are okay with me sharing and how it will be shared. In private conversations, however, I rely on the discernment of the Holy Spirit.

For instance, our son's mental health issues, which have included suicide attempts, commitment to a mental hospital on several occasions, and homelessness, have greatly affected our lives as parents. He has graciously allowed me to talk publicly about his story. But even if he didn't give me permission to do so, my closest friends who encourage me and pray for me and my family would know. If God opened the door, there also might be one-on-one conversations I would still have with another mom who is walking a similar journey with her own child.

When Mark and I began healing from his affair, we talked about what we were comfortable sharing. We agreed we could have one-on-one conversations with our close circle of friends and anyone we felt would benefit from our story. However, we agreed we would not talk about it publicly until we were further down the healing road. It was three years before we both agreed to share about it publicly.

Most people don't have a "public" life they need to worry about, so something like that might not apply to you. However, committing to keep a secret that isolates you from the help you need or the help you can give is not an emotionally healthy promise for you to make. You are not meant to walk through life isolated. Don't make a commitment to isolate yourself. Do make a commitment to honor your loved one when you speak about your story that's also their story. Most importantly, focus on how *you* felt, what *you* learned, and how God grew *you* through it. Then it's far more *your* story than anyone else's story.

I'm so open that it seems I scare people away. How can I find the right balance of when to share my story? Sometimes it's perfectly okay to share that "you understand" with a complete stranger, giving them little pieces of your story to let them know they're not alone. It's appropriate because it's what's first on their mind and you might be able to give them hope and encouragement. However, in everyday friendships, you'll want to wait to share experience stories until either the right time (she shares about tough stuff in her marriage, which gives you the opportunity to share tough stuff you've walked through) or until a foundation of trust has been built.

When we tend to share our experience stories too quickly too often, it's usually good to evaluate our motive. Be honest with yourself. Are you looking for pity or trying to make yourself look good for overcoming difficult circumstances? If so, you need to wait for a more appropriate time to share your story when your heart is in the right place. Are you depending on your story to give you value? Remember, your value is determined by God, not your circumstances. Wait to share until you're feeling solid in who really gives you value.

More than anything, it's important to remember that, as Christians, our stories are really not about us at all. They're about our God and what He's done in us through our story. That's always the right motive for sharing!

I'm worried about gossip. How can I make sure someone is trustworthy? There's always risk involved when sharing your story. We're dealing with imperfect human beings here!

It's possible someone you share your story with decides to share it with someone else as she's walking through her own similar situation. It's possible a friend isn't as trustworthy as you originally thought. It's possible a friendship will go rogue and your story will be in the hands of someone with whom you no longer interact. It's also possible and entirely probable that God is bigger than any of those situations.

There are two psalms that are powerful reminders of allowing God to be our Defender and Protector. Psalm 91:1–2 assures us that "He who dwells in the shelter of the Most High will abide in the shadow of the Almighty. I will say to the LORD, '"My refuge and my fortress, my God, in whom I trust.'" Psalm 18:1–3 declares, "I love you, O LORD, my strength. The LORD is my rock and my fortress and my deliverer, my God, my rock, in whom I take refuge, my shield, and the horn of my salvation, my stronghold. I call upon the LORD, who is worthy to be praised, and I am saved from my enemies."

We have to trust that God will use everything that happens to us for His good. That's a promise made in Romans 8:28: "And we know that God causes everything to work together for the good of those who love God and are called according to his purpose for them" (NLT). Can you let go and trust that God will still make good come out of something you can't control?

I'm worried about what people will think. Most of us are, to some degree. We want people to think well of us and those that mean the most to us. What I've learned, however, is that respect increases when vulnerability deepens. Particularly if you can humbly share what God taught you or is teaching you through the journey.

How do I know when it's the right time for me to share my story? There's a difference between sharing when you're "in process" and sharing when healing has started. We need a friend or two with whom we can process difficulties. However, when we're sharing for the purpose of helping someone else, we want to at least be on the healing side of the issue. We don't have to be completely healed but at least far enough along to identify lessons learned.

SHARING LEADS TO PRAYING

When we share our stories, we enable others to pray with and for us. When we hear someone's story, we know better how to pray with and for her. We're better together when we're on our knees for each other. Turn the page and let's look at the power of praying together.

FROM ANNE'S HEART

When Landon was four months old, we began to notice he was incredibly thin. Come to find out he had actually dropped below his birth weight. He was sleeping all the time and was never content. We discovered I wasn't producing enough milk to sustain him and he was labeled "failure to thrive." We instantly switched to formula and he began to flourish.

Mommy guilt.

I look back at pictures and think, "How could I not have noticed? Landon was essentially starving and I didn't know."

Mommy guilt.

Between a new baby diagnosed with "failure to thrive," an active two-year-old, and everyday things that needed to be done, I spiraled deep into the baby blues. Honestly, it took me almost two years to finally feel normal again. It was an incredibly hard season for my marriage and family.

Mommy guilt.

Mommy guilt is real! It has a way of eating at the soul because we often battle it silently, allowing Satan to whisper his lies of ineptitude into our hearts as moms.

It wasn't until I started opening up about the struggles I was facing in my journey that I began receiving encouragement and support. It's also when I began hearing, "Me too!" Talk about relief to know you aren't the only mom who forgets to buckle her child into their seat or has to battle daily to rein in anxiety.

As someone who struggles with depression, it is so easy to lose sight of the fact that God doesn't see me through that lens. He sees me as His daughter created with a purpose, and He hurts when I hurt. He sees you the same way!

It takes honesty, transparency, and guts to share our stories. When we take the plunge into vulnerability, we experience freedom from mommy guilt and a deeper community.

SOMETHING TO THINK ABOUT . . .

What have you been experiencing mommy guilt about? Can you muster up the courage to share and walk toward freedom?

Today's Friendship Assignment

Choose one of these to do today:

1) Think through and jot down your experience stories. This is a first step to sharing your stories.

2) If your story is leaking out in ways that are not relationally helpful, take the next step into healing and hope. Contact a friend, a pastor, or a counselor to help you unpack your story.

3) Ask God to show you someone who needs to hear your experience story. Then be brave and share it to give her hope and help.

## CHAPTER 8

Praying Together
"I'm standing in the gap for you."

Prayer. That word alone can launch fear or faith in a mom's heart. Fear if you don't know how to pray. Faith if it comes easy to you. Fear if you think that God is too big or too busy to hear your prayers. Faith if you know He's always available and waiting to hear from you. Fear if you worry about saying the right things. Faith if you just pour out your heart without giving "how you say it" any thought. Fear if you think God won't answer your prayers, faith if you trust He loves you and will answer in the best way for you. Our goal on these next few pages is to help every mom who's joining us on this *Better Together* journey to exchange any prayer uncertainty with prayer confidence. Girlfriend, you are not only better doing life together with other moms, but you are better doing life together with God!

Let's start with one basic tenet of truth: There's nothing fancy about prayer. In fact, there's no "right" or "wrong" way to pray! Prayer is simply having a conversation with God. Sometimes those conversations are slow and thoughtful. Sometimes they are quick and grow out of pure desperation.

You are not only better doing life together with other moms, but you are better doing life together with God!

In a mom's world those prayers may happen at 3 a.m. (please, God, I need this kid to sleep so I can sleep) or sitting on the toilet (Lord, I just need two minutes to myself!) or staring out a window when your teen is past curfew (God, I need Your peace that passes understanding right now). Other times they happen when you're watching your kids play well and you whisper a prayer of thanks. Or you wake up a few minutes before the kids wake up or use your lunch hour or the first few minutes of naptime to spend a little time with God. We all know, though, quiet moments are few and far between for a mom who's smack-dab in the middle of raising a family!

IT STARTS WITH YOU

I picked up the phone and dialed the number on the brochure to see if there was a Moms In Prayer (then known as Moms In Touch) group at my daughter's school. The literature my husband had picked up at a conference indicated that these groups gathered for one hour a week to pray for their children and their school. The woman who answered told me there wasn't a group for that school yet, would I be interested in starting one? I wasn't prepared for that question. I mumbled something about not having any idea what you could possibly pray about for an hour. She chuckled and said, "If you gather the moms, I'll teach you how to pray." I told her she had a deal.

Praying in a Moms In Prayer group was one of the best experiences for expanding my prayer life. Up to that point in my life, prayer was an occasional thought that was almost always in desperation. Being involved in Moms In Prayer taught me to slow down and spend time with God, pray Scripture, and keep track of prayer requests and answered prayers. It introduced me to different ways to talk with God (praise Him, ask for forgiveness from Him, thank Him, and lift up my needs to Him) and how to turn my worries into prayers. It also increased my comfort level in praying with others. (Check out www.momsinprayer.org to find a group near you!)

Some of my friends have had a similar experience through different groups. My friend Jen became more comfortable with prayer in a Bible study her church offered. Sue was a part of Community Bible Study (www.communitybiblestudy.org) and Kelly found that Bible Study Fellowship (www.bsfinternational.org) was a key player in strengthening her faith and prayer life. Not only do these kinds of groups and studies help deepen our foundation in God's truth and prayer, but they also widen our MBF (Might Be Friends) circle. Having friends who are strong in their faith brings a strength to our own lives.

Better Together is about having successful mom relationships. Our mom relationships will be better if we intentionally deepen our friendship with God. Why? Because the more we hang out with God, the more we become like Him. We learn to forgive, give grace, be patient, be bold, reach out, share hope, and see others through the eyes of Jesus. We're able to love deeper and experience a joy and peace that are not dependent upon our circumstances. These Christlike characteristics not only help us to be a better friend, but they also help us to navigate the sometimes-rocky water of relationships. Do you want to improve your friendships? It's best to invest also in your friendship with God. How do you do that? It comes down to truth and talking.

TRUTH

Anne loves Romans 15:13 (NLT), "I pray that God, the source of hope, will fill you completely with joy and peace because you trust in him. Then you will overflow with confident hope through the power of the Holy Spirit." She shared, "I love this picture! My family can experience God's confident hope in the *overflow* of joy and peace He provides. How does one get filled with the promised joy and peace? By spending time with God, taking care of ourselves, nurturing our marriage, and nurturing our children (in that order)." Friendships fall in the "taking care of ourselves" category, so I think it's important to note that investing in our friendship with God and investing in our friendship with others needs to be a priority in our lives. Doing so will help us be the wife and mom we want to be.

How does a busy mom find time to spend with God? As a mom of littles, Anne writes Bible verses on index cards and posts the verses all through her house. There's a verse on each bathroom mirror, on a couple of kitchen cabinets, and even in her car. My friend Cheri finds connection listening to worship music throughout the day. When my kids were small, I kept a Bible in each bathroom and one in my car to use during the many hours of waiting at piano lessons, doctor appointments, and soccer practice. Today our smartphones allow us to carry the Bible with us anywhere we go. There are also great devotional apps and even apps that help us keep track of prayer requests and favorite Bible verses. Here are some helpful tips for making time with God a priority:

1) *Keep a "God Time" basket by your favorite chair.* Tuck your Bible, your devotional (if you use one), a notebook and pen, index cards, and maybe even stationery note cards in the basket. Then everything is at your fingertips whenever you decide to spend some time with God. (The note cards are suggested so you can write a note of encouragement to someone God brought to mind during your time with Him.)

2) *Read big or read small.* There are many approaches on "how" to read the Bible. There's no one right way; it's just important to read it! However, if you don't know where to start, you can try one of two ways: Go big or go small.

If you go big, you'll be choosing one of the sixty-six books of the Bible to read over a period of time, reading just one or two chapters a day. (If your goal is to read the whole Bible and you read one chapter a day, it will take you three years and three months to get all the way through!)

If you go small, you'll choose one verse to focus on. If you choose one verse, you'll read it daily for a period of time, turn it into a prayer, memorize it, and talk about it with a friend, your spouse, or your kids. You might write it on an index card or two, put it as the background on your phone, or find other creative ways to keep it in front of you as much as possible. You can focus on one verse a week. You can add to your understanding of that verse by looking up other verses on the same subject. If your Bible offers cross-reference verses, you can look those up too. Other ideas for digging into God's Word include

• *Studying a particular book of the Bible.* Some great books to start with include Psalms, Proverbs, Matthew, Mark, Luke, John, Romans, Philippians, Galatians, Ephesians, and James. You can find online commentaries or Bible studies that will ask questions to help you think through and apply what you're reading.

• *Using a devotional.* There are many devotionals out there for moms or marriage. They usually offer a story and a verse to get you headed in the right direction. Check out the *No More Perfect Moms* devotional on the You Version Bible App!

• *Reading a Proverb a day.* There are thirty-one chapters in Proverbs and each month has anywhere from twenty-eight to thirty-one days. If you read the Proverb chapter that corresponds to the day of the month, you'll read the entire book of Proverbs in a month. Then you can start over again the next month! You can never read the wisdom of Proverbs too often!

• *Reading a book that is also a Bible study.* Hearts at Home's *Real Moms . . . Real Jesus* is a book that will deepen your friendship with Jesus while also having you read through the book of Matthew.

• *Choose a predetermined Bible reading plan to follow.* At websites like www.biblegateway.com and in apps like You Version Bible App, you can find all kinds of Bible reading plans. You can find plans to read the Bible in thirty days or two years. There are plans that allow you to read the Bible chronologically, or focus just on the New Testament or the Old Testament. Find a plan that interests you and dive in!

• *Following a topical study.* Think of a particular area where you need encouragement. Faith, hope, trust, temptation, and fear are common topics people look to the Bible for wisdom. Using a concordance (a type of Bible index) or searching for those words in your Bible app or online Bible will allow you to find all the Bible verses on that topic.

• *Writing in your Bible.* It isn't sacrilegious to write in your Bible! Our time with God (which happens when we talk to Him and read His Word) is supposed to be a living, breathing, interactive relationship. As you read God's Word, you might make note of the date you read a chapter. You could also note the date when you shared a verse with a friend or family member. You can take notes in your Bible during a sermon at church. You can write thoughts as you read, underlining verses that seem to pop out on the page at you.

> *God often communicates through His people. That is why it's valuable to have spiritually strong friends.*

Anytime you build friendships that have a spiritual connection, you'll have opportunity to share what God is teaching you, talk about what you're reading in your Bible, and offer one another accountability for staying in God's Word. Sometimes when I find a Bible verse that gives me a "wow" or addresses something a friend is going through, I'll text the verse to my friend. This keeps me interacting with my friend and the Word!

TALKING

Prayer is simply talking to God. We need to hear from God and He needs to hear from us. When it comes to hearing from God, you're probably like me wishing that God would just open up the heavens and announce with a big booming voice the direction He wants me to take! It doesn't work that way, but we do hear from God in three different ways:

1) *Through His Word:* Romans 10:17 tells us that "faith comes from hearing, and hearing through the word of Christ." When Mark chose to leave for three months, I was reading the book of Romans. I'd been asking God for direction on how I was to interact with Mark but hadn't seemed to get any answers. One day I was reading Romans 12:9–21, and I knew in that moment God had answered my prayer: "Let love be genuine. Abhor what is evil; hold fast to what is good. Love one another with brotherly affection. Outdo one another in showing honor. Do not be slothful in zeal, be fervent in spirit, serve the Lord. Rejoice in hope, be patient in tribulation, be constant in prayer. Contribute to the needs of the saints and seek to show hospitality. Bless those who persecute you; bless and do not curse them. Rejoice with those who rejoice, weep with those who weep. Live in harmony with one another. Do not be haughty, but associate with the lowly. Never be wise in your own sight. Repay no one evil for evil, but give thought to do what is honorable in the sight of all. If possible, so far as it depends on you, live peaceably with all. Beloved, never avenge yourselves, but leave it to the

> *I* was seven years old and so was she when we met. Forty-one years later we are still friends. I live in Illinois and Melissa lives in New Jersey. I was there when her first child was born (her own mom died when we were young) so I was able to help. When my husband died almost a year ago, she flew in to be by my side. I recently attended her daughter's high school graduation. We see each other once a year in Ohio at my parents' house. I could not do life without her.—MICHELLE

wrath of God, for it is written, 'Vengeance is mine, I will repay, says the Lord.' To the contrary, if your enemy is hungry, feed him; if he is thirsty, give him something to drink; for by so doing you will heap burning coals on his head. Do not be overcome by evil, but overcome evil with good." This was the exact direction I needed. I did my best to live it out.

When I shared that passage with Mark after he returned home, he said, "Oh my goodness! You did that! You were kind even when I wasn't. You really did heap burning coals on my head!"

2) *Through God's people.* Proverbs 15:22 (NIV) tells us, "Plans fail for lack of counsel, but with many advisers they succeed." God often communicates through His people. This is why it is valuable to have spiritually strong friends. When seeking wisdom, it's also important to get confirmation from several believers. "By the mouth of two or three witnesses every fact may be confirmed" (Matthew 18:16 NASB). Remember, God will never contradict Himself. If anyone ever gives you direction to do something against God's Word, that's a red flag that He is not using them to speak to you. God also speaks words of encouragement to us through our friends. When I was in the midst of cancer treatment, many friends emailed or texted Bible verses to me. I drank in those words from God via my friends as they were refreshing water to my dry soul.

3) *Through the Holy Spirit.* John 14:15–17 confirms the Holy Spirit's role in leading and guiding. "I will talk to the Father, and he'll provide you another Friend so that you will always have someone with you. This Friend is the Spirit of Truth. The godless world can't take him in because it doesn't have eyes to see him, doesn't know what to look for. But you know him already because he has been staying with you, and will even

be *in* you!" (THE MESSAGE). The Holy Spirit is our Helper. Our Guide. Our always present Friend. Those little internal nudges we get (that are in line with the Bible!) are often the Holy Spirit guiding us in the right direction. One morning I woke up and just knew I needed to send my friend Michele a certain Bible verse. Although we lived nearly a thousand miles apart, we had both walked through cancer together via technology. I looked up the verse (it was Romans 15:13) on my Bible app, copied it into a text message, and pressed send. Within a minute she wrote back, "How did you know I needed this?" I said, "Well I didn't, but God did." She responded, "Thank you for that. Found out the cancer is back more aggressive this time . . . Thank you for listening to God's whisper." That's the Holy Spirit! I can't say that I've always heard those whispers or recognized those nudges, but when I do, I am always amazed at how God leads.

In the same way we need to hear from God, He also needs to hear from us. Praying is like talking to your BFF. It's easy to talk to someone when you know they love you unconditionally! Think about your conversations with a friend: Sometimes you give her a pat on the back, sometimes you apologize, sometimes you thank her, sometimes you fill her in on your life letting her know what you need, and still sometimes you're quiet, listening to her heart. Those are the same conversations we need to be having with God! God WANTS to hear from us wherever we are in our faith journey no matter if we're in a good place spiritually or in a hard place!

Need to know some practical ways to talk with God? Sometimes a great place to start is by praying and personalizing the actual Bible verses we read. Simply add your name or your friend's name (or your spouse or child's name) to a Scripture. Here are some examples:

• Isaiah 12:2, "I will trust, and will not be afraid; for the LORD GOD is my strength and my song," can become "I pray that _____ will trust in You for You are her strength and her song."

• Proverbs 3:5–6, "Trust in the LORD with all your heart, and do not lean on your own understanding. In all your ways acknowledge him, and he will make straight your paths," can become "I pray that _____ will trust you with her whole heart and resist the urge to try to humanly make sense of this. May she acknowledge You and allow You to guide her."

• 2 Thessalonians 3:16, "Now may the Lord of peace himself give you peace at all times in every way. The Lord be with you all," can become "Lord, _____ needs Your peace. I pray she feels Your presence right now."

Praying Scripture is a beautiful way to blend prayer and God's Word. It's a power-packed Bible-centered tool in our spiritual toolbox. Using a pattern for prayer is another helpful tool. Years ago a mentor shared an easy way for me to remember these conversations: ACTS. A-Adoration, C-Confession, T-Thanksgiving, S-Supplication. I eventually added an extra S-Silence. This acronym is actually created from the pattern of prayer Jesus gave us in what we know today as the Lord's Prayer. This prayer wasn't really designed for us to recite as much as it was to give us a picture of how to talk with God. These are great conversations to have with God:

Adoration—God, I praise You because You are _____
(faithful, trustworthy, truth, hope, peace, all-knowing, all-powerful, etc.).

Confession—Lord, I'm so sorry for _____.
Will You please forgive me?

Thanksgiving—Father God, thank You for _____.

Supplication—Lord, I'm asking for Your help with

_____. (Supplication comes from the word "supply." It's asking God to supply all our needs.) This is also when we pray for the needs of others.

Silence—Too often we talk more than we listen. Sometimes we simply need to sit in awe of God. Sometimes we need to calm our anxious heart by simply being with him. Psalm 46:10 reminds us to "be still, and know that I am God." During this time of silence, I usually keep a pen and paper close by because God prompts all kinds of things like remembering to call a friend, prompting me to pull something out of the freezer for dinner, or reminding me it's a friend's birthday today.

Hebrews 4:16 (NLT) reminds us to "come boldly to the throne of our gracious God. There we will receive his mercy, and we will find grace to help us when we need it." We need to talk with God with respect, reverence, and awe but also with the familiarity of a friend.

SPENDING TIME WITH GOD . . . YOUR WAY!

You and I need to BE praying friends and we need to HAVE praying friends. We need to stand in the gap for each other. Sometimes we need to simply take over in praying during hard seasons.

I once noticed a Facebook status Julie Barnhill posted. She was asking if there were some weary mommas out there who have been praying for their kiddos who are walking in the wrong direction and are weary, not knowing what else to pray. She encouraged them to partner with another momma who can intercede in a fresh way. I thought the suggestion was brilliant. Sometimes when we just don't know what else to pray, we need a friend to stand in the gap. Don't have a friend like that? Take the first step and ask a friend if she'd like to link arms with you to pray for each other's family. You can meet regularly or just shoot each other texts, emails, or even Snapchats to share requests!

There are many needs out there, and sometimes we need a way to keep them correlated to your organizational style. Innies thrive on prayer journals. They love the organized sections of a journal, filling up the lined paper and writing an organized list of prayer requests. An outie might love the idea of a prayer journal but when she has a half-dozen abandoned prayer journals in her possession, she may find herself frustrated and even feeling like a failure. There's no right or wrong way to pray or keep your prayer life organized. My "outiness" finds that sticky notes work far better for me than a journal. Another mom I know uses a smartphone app for organizing her prayer requests. She prays daily for her husband and kids and critical timely needs (a friend's doctor appointment that day or her nephew's surgery recovery) and then prays through different needs on certain weekdays: Monday is missionaries, Tuesday is friends, Wednesday is her church leadership, Thursday is extended family, and Friday she prays for her kids' teachers.

I once visited a mom who decided to create a literal prayer closet out of an extra unused shower (I know . . . who has an unused shower? But she did!). She put a pillow on the floor to kneel on, had her Bible open on the built-in "seat" in the shower, and sticky notes all over the walls. Some stickies were Bible verses, others were people's names, and some were inspiring quotes. This mama took "go into your prayer closet" (Matthew 6:6) to a whole new level! That's not necessarily what you or I should do. We need to do what works for us, but we can be inspired by her ingenuity.

I recently met a mom who is very creative. She often uses a sketch pad and pencils or even paints during her quiet times. No lined pages for this girl; she's being true to herself and finding ways to enhance her time with God using her artistic gift. Figuring out how to best talk to God helps us to be the praying friend someone is likely praying for!

PRAYING INSTEAD OF PROMISING

We've all done it: promised someone we'd pray for them and completely forgotten to follow through. Our intentions are honorable, but life is busy and we just forget. How about a different strategy? Let's pray instead of promising to pray!

When a friend messages you on Facebook and asks you to pray for her, instead of telling her you will, just type a prayer right there in Facebook Messenger. Get a text from a friend going through a hard time? Respond with a prayer texted back to her. Standing in the church lobby following a worship service and your friend mentions her son's upcoming surgery and asks you to pray? Respond with, "Let me pray for you right now." Talking with a friend on the phone and she mentions an upcoming parent-teacher conference she wants you to be praying for? Tell her, "Let's pray about that now."

If you're not accustomed to praying spontaneously like that, it may feel awkward the first time you do it, and maybe even the second. But each time will build up your confidence and courage until praying for someone "in the moment" is your normal response. No more forgetting to pray. "Do it and do it now" can be your new prayer motto!

You can apply a similar strategy to praying in groups. So often we spend more time sharing prayer requests than actually praying. If you want everyone to give an update on their life, by all means spend time talking and give everyone time to share. Rather than sharing prayer requests, you can have people pray their requests and then others in the group will join in to pray for them. At Hearts at Home we call this kind of praying in a group "popcorn prayer," because we're simply popping all over the group, praying aloud as the Holy Spirit leads. Usually, before we begin praying, we identify who will close the prayer time, but up until that the floor is open for anyone to pipe in and pray. No need for long-winded prayers here either. A single sentence followed by another person's single-sentence prayer works just fine. No fancy language. Make sure you resist the urge to feel like you don't pray "well enough." That's just the enemy's scheme to keep you quiet—and you're not going to let him win!

I remember Mom stopping, putting her hand on my shoulder as I held my purple lunch box, and praying.

While I was writing this chapter, my friend Becky texted me this powerful verse from Nehemiah 4:13–14: "So I stationed armed guards at the most vulnerable places of the wall and assigned people by families with their swords, lances, and bows. After looking things over I stood up and spoke to the nobles, officials, and everyone else: 'Don't be afraid of them. Put your minds on the Master, great and awesome, and then fight for your brothers, your sons, your daughters, your wives, and your homes'" (THE MESSAGE). What a reminder of why we pray! There are vulnerable places in our lives we need to protect with prayer. In doing so, we put our minds on the Master and fight for our brothers, sisters, sons, daughters, spouses, and families!

We pray for one another because lives are at stake. Families are on the battlefield. Marriages are crumbling. We pray to stand in the gap for our kids and our friends' kids. We pray to get out of the way and let God do the work. We pray to hand over the reins of our own heart when we're tempted to take matters in our own hands. We pray with and for one another because when we do, we really are better together.

FROM ANNE'S HEART

It has become a tradition of sorts that I serve as my mom's personal assistant at the National Hearts At Home Conference. I love spending that time with her! One aspect of the job is standing in front of a workshop to introduce her and pray. I stepped out onto the stage and did just that, thinking nothing of it. A few friends grabbed me afterward and said, "We can't believe you prayed! Out loud! To a large group of women!" I chuckled because it is second nature for me, and I have my parents to thank for that.

One of the first times I remember Mom praying out loud for me, I was around third grade. I am not sure if I was having a hard time or what, but I remember Mom stopping, putting her hand on my shoulder as I held my purple lunch box, and praying. I don't remember the words, but the moment is imprinted on my heart.

I now know that was not an easy thing for my mom to do. She and my dad were learning how to make spontaneous prayer a "new normal" for our family. When she teaches about prayer, she often says, "You've got to push through awkward to get to a new normal." When she prayed for me in third grade, it felt awkward to her! But she pushed through it and now our family finds praying together a "normal" thing to do!

My daughter, Rilyn, can be quite dramatic. She loves making videos of her talking, singing, dancing, or doing all three. I recently found a video she had created on my computer and I couldn't help but soak in the gift of the moment as I listened to her say, "Know what? My heart feels good for you and God. I need to pray for you." And just like that she began praying for whoever it was she was making the video for.

Because my mom decided to step out of her comfort zone twenty years ago and learn to pray, it has become inherent for the next two generations. If prayer isn't a natural part of your life but you'd like it to be, I encourage you to just do it. Something as simple as "Lord, I need You" is a great place to start. Consider the faith you'd like your children to have and start living that way yourself. You never know how your step of faith could impact future generations!

SOMETHING TO THINK ABOUT:

*What part of friendship or prayer is awkward
to you? What "awkward" do you need to
push through to get to a new normal?*

Today's Friendship Assignment

Do you have a friend going through a tough time?
Pray for her via text.

Are you going through a tough time? Ask a friend to
partner in prayer with you.

Stop for two minutes and talk with God before you
turn to the next chapter.

## CHAPTER 9

Forgiving Together
"I'm sorry, I let you down."

"I'm sorry, we can't be friends anymore," she said to me after we sat down with our cups of tea at the coffee shop she had invited me to. I completely thought she was kidding. As the conversation continued, I realized she wasn't. I asked her why and she could give no reason, simply saying that she just wasn't a good friend. I begged her to give me some understanding of what had happened to cause her to feel that way. *She can't be serious,* I thought. Within ten minutes our time together was over, seven years of friendship were tossed aside, and my heart was absolutely broken. I'd never experienced a friendship breakup. I wasn't even sure they really happened. That day I found out they do.

Friends bring a lot to our lives. They strengthen us. They deepen our faith. They laugh and cry with us. Sometimes they serve us or serve with us. They listen. They challenge. They share their hearts. They help us when we're down and celebrate with us when things are going well. Our lives are better when we mom together.

Yet linking arms with a friend is linking arms with an imperfect human being. You will likely let each other down and need to navigate some conflict along the way. Occasionally, you may experience a gradual distance in a relationship and have to make a decision whether to fight for the friendship. Friends will move and you'll likely experience loss. It's possible you'll discover a relationship is toxic and need to make a decision to put some healthy distance between you and a friend. You might even experience a "breakup" as I did.

> *Linking arms with a friend is linking arms with an imperfect human being.*

Then we add in our own fears and emotions. We're fearful a friend could hurt us. We're afraid trust might be broken or someone will betray or abandon us. We can easily personalize something a friend says and feel hurt. We may experience the rejection of disapproval if a friend doesn't agree with a choice we make.

Knowing all this, is friendship worth it? You bet! Relationships take work, but that work is not only worth it, it actually benefits us!

PUT ON YOUR BIG-GIRL PANTIES

I remember when my girls were potty-training and they were so excited to wear big-girl panties! That step meant they were becoming big girls and moving further from toddler status. They were maturing, growing, and learning how to take care of themselves in new ways.

Relationships do the same for us. Both the good and hard parts of friendships teach us lessons, stretch us, and mature us in communication, conflict, vulnerability, courage, and wisdom. Friendships are neither simple nor effortless. They require us to dig deep and work hard to create relationships that go the distance. If we're honest with ourselves, the challenges of friendships help us put on our big-girl panties! Navigating the challenging side of friendships can be approached in two ways: proactively and reactively. Let's explore both of these on the next few pages.

PREVENTING FRIENDSHIP FRUSTRATIONS

Friendship requires the effort of two people. Evaluating your own friendship lens is an important place to start. Proactively, there are three "preventing conflict and disappointment" strategies you can implement in your relationships.

Watch your expectations. Sometimes our own expectations trip us up in friendships. Maybe we expect friendship to just "happen" without work. Or maybe we expect to be someone's only friend or best friend. It's possible we take a friend for granted, expecting the relationship to just exist for the long haul without investing in it. Maybe we expect the other person to make the effort and we forget it's a two-way street. Perhaps we throw our whole self into relationships and expect others to do the same, at an almost unrealistic level. We might put our friendship on a pedestal, expecting more than any relationship could ever deliver. In fact, we might have an unrealistic expectation for a friend to fill a God-shaped void in our heart. If you've had trouble being satisfied with friendships, expectation management could be a first place to start making some important changes.

Clarify expectations. It's okay to be clear about what you can or cannot do. My friend Becky has been wonderful to strip expectations away. She says, "I enjoy when we do connect; there's no guilt when we don't." I'm so appreciative of how she's clarified her expectations of how often we connect as friends. Becky says, "No-guilt friendship is so needed. Guilt is a big problem in friendship and can keep people from reconnecting after lapses in communication, missing a birthday, etc. Releasing a friend from the guilt piece is a gift."

If you dislike talking on the phone, tell your friend that! Don't get frustrated when she calls you all the time. Tell her you prefer to text or spend time together, but you're not one to talk on the phone much. This helps clear up confusion about your differing approaches to connecting!

We might have an unrealistic expectation for a friend to fill a God-shaped void in our heart.

Be intentional about your own emotional health. Be honest with yourself. Do you easily get jealous in friendships? Do you have trouble being happy for a friend when something good happens to her? Are you insecure? Struggle with your identity? Are you clingy in relationships? Resist vulnerability? Are you demanding? Are you expecting a friendship to fill a void of unsatisfied needs? Do you have trouble trusting? Do you tend to stay distant from people because you don't want to let them down? Sometimes what we didn't receive from our parents in terms of love, affection, support, and direction, we will project onto others. We expect our friends (or our spouse or children) to provide what we're still yearning for from childhood. Each of these issues and others like them can eventually make an appearance in friendships. They cause us to look at some parts of relationships through a lens that doesn't always tell us the truth.

When an emotional health issue appears, don't brush it off. Don't rationalize it away. Deal with it. Talk to God about it. Talk to your friend about it. If necessary, find a counselor who can help you sort through, understand, and move beyond it. Most importantly, do the internal work you know needs to be done, for your sake and for the sake of your relationships.

DEALING WITH FRIENDSHIP FRUSTRATIONS

It's happened. Somehow there's misunderstanding, distance, or hurt feelings between you and a friend. The temptation is to run away, or talk to someone other than your friend, or put your head in the sand and pretend everything is okay. While those are all natural responses, they're not "big-girl panty" options. So what do we do? These seven principles can help you deal with the inevitable friendship foul:

Check your heart. What assumptions are you making about your friend's intentions? Just because something made you feel disrespected, intimidated, or misunderstood doesn't mean she intended any of those feelings to happen. Don't assume your perspective is right and her perspective is wrong. Ask God to show you any place where you need to do an attitude adjustment as it pertains to this particular friendship.

Talk only to her. When we're looking for wisdom, the best place to start is the Bible. God has a thing or two to say about conflict. One of the best places is Matthew 18:15 (NIV), "If your brother or sister sins, go and point out their fault, just between the two of you." Notice that it doesn't say, "If your sister sins against you, go and tell three other girlfriends what she did." The important words for us to focus on are "just between the two of you." All too often there's a simple misunderstanding that can be solved with a single conversation. Share your thoughts or concerns in order to move forward in your friendship. Some great phrases to start these conversations are:

- Can we sort through what happened this morning?

- Can you help me understand . . . ?

- I need your help with what just happened. Do you have a few minutes to talk?

- I think we have different perspectives about _____. I'd like to hear your thoughts on this.

- Can you help me understand what you meant when you said _____?

Talk soon. "Do not let the sun go down on your anger" are the words of wisdom found in Ephesians 4:26b. While you might not be able to live out those words literally, the takeaway is to resolve issues sooner rather than later. When you wait to deal with something, it often grows bigger in your head and heart than it needs to be, growing into unresolved bitterness. The gap between you and your friend becomes a gaping hole you can see, but she has no idea it exists!

Keep the big picture in mind. Your goal is a deeper, stronger relationship. You want to try to untangle this issue and better understand each other so you don't trip over it again. This isn't about confronting . . . it's about communicating honestly. In Proverbs 27:6 (NKJV) King Solomon wrote, "Faithful are the wounds of a friend, but the kisses of an enemy are deceitful." The "wounds of a friend" are when a friend tells us something hard to hear, but it helps us in the long run. We don't usually think of the words "wounds of a friend" as being positive, but we need our friends to be honest with us!

Be empathetic. Try to see your friend's point of view. Don't assume she even sees the issue the same way you do. Seek to understand before seeking to be understood.

Be loving. You may have grown up in a family where you "tell it like it is," raise your voice, or enjoy spirited debate. She, on the other hand, may have grown up in a family that swept conflict under the rug. Be loving, gentle, and kind in your conversation, making it safe for both of you to share your thoughts and find resolve.

All too often there's a simple misunderstanding that can be solved with a single conversation.

Bring resolution to the table. Own what you can own. Apologize for what you can apologize for. Ask for and offer forgiveness. Even if you feel you're only 5 percent wrong and she's 95 percent wrong, own your 5 percent. If you set the pace on that, she will likely follow. Remember the big picture is to resolve the conflict and strengthen your friendship!

Friendships need to be tended to, cared for, and nurtured. When a friendship hits a speed bump, that's our reminder to slow down, take time to talk, recommit, and hopefully move the friendship forward. Occasionally, however, there are times when friendships fail.

FRIENDSHIP FIASCOS

In a perfect world, all our friendships would work out. There would be no conflict, no frustration, and no failed relationships. We don't live in a perfect world so unfortunately we'll all experience some friendship fiascos along the way.

As honorable as it is to protect and preserve a friendship, there will likely be times we need to let one go. Most of us hate to see that happen, but we need to know that it's normal, it's okay, and at times it's even healthy.

Sometimes we have to remember there are people with whom we're "worse together."

A friend may call it quits because of her own capacity for relationships. She may feel she just can't invest in so many relationships. A friendship may end because the commonalities that drew you together no longer exist. For instance, you were both attending the same church and now one of you has changed churches. You no longer "live the same church life" and the relationship naturally experiences distance. A friend may close the friendship door because she just doesn't feel the same way about the friendship she did years ago. Her friendship needs have changed.

It was Henry Wadsworth Longfellow who said, "Great is the art of the beginning, but greater is the art of ending." Some friendships are lifetime connections while others are given to us for a season. Because you have a limited emotional bank and only so many hours in a day, it's okay to fine-tune your friendship circle. Some relationships naturally fade, and that's okay. Life evolves. Friendships fade and new friendships bloom. It's not uncommon for friendships to experience friend-shifts. You'll probably always care about each other, but there are times you may need to accept that a relationship has run its course. It's only natural that friendships change as motherhood changes.

If your friendship plate is full, it's okay to choose carefully which relationships are worth investing in. While many fades happen naturally, you might intentionally fade a friendship by moving your daily texts to several times a week. If your life plate is full, however, don't let your friendships fade because you simply don't have time for them. Remember, you're not designed to do life alone!

It's entirely possible during the TBF phase that you'll discover someone isn't who you thought they would be. Or, you might find that your longtime friend's new home business that she feels you need to be part of is putting a wedge between the two of you. You've talked to her about it, but nothing is changing. These situations and others like them may indicate it's time to intentionally end a friendship. If you're in the TBF phase, you may be able to back off your efforts to connect. Sometimes even GGF relationships can naturally fade. If, however, you've been longtime friends, you may need to have a conversation letting her know how much you've appreciated having her in your life, but the way the two of you relate to

TBF—TRYING TO BE FRIENDS

MBF—MIGHT BE FRIENDS

GGF—GOOD GIRLFRIEND

BFF—BEST FRIEND FOREVER

each other isn't healthy for either one of you. This gives the relationship closure and is honoring to your friend.

Friendships are intended to have a healthy balance between give and take. They need to contribute positively and bring a joy to our lives. Sometimes, however, we have to realize there are people with whom we're "worse together." Toxic friendships are draining, unsupportive, and often unequal. We give, give, give, and they take, take, take. Of course, there are times where one friend is in a receiving season because of crisis or life circumstances. That's not a toxic relationship because it will return to a balance in time. A toxic relationship regularly brings us down or consistently takes without giving.

If a friendship starts out healthy but becomes toxic, a conversation with your friend is probably the best place to start. This gives her the benefit of feedback and the opportunity to make changes. Most toxic friends are either emotionally unhealthy or emotionally immature. Some respond to feedback and truly want to make changes while others just can't seem to make the needed changes to make a friendship truly successful. When that happens, you have two choices. One is to end the friendship, knowing that this is hurting you and you need to stop the hurt. The other is to choose to still be a friend,

I met my BFF Kristi at a conference where we were matched up with roommates we didn't know. After the conference, she sent me an email. I answered, and a few weeks later, got another email. Before long it was an email or two every day, then instant messaging, and phone calls. It was a friendship made in heaven! Eleven years later, she's my best friend and I have no idea what I'd do without her!—BECKY

limit your time together, establish healthy boundaries, and make a conscious decision to have few to no expectations of the other person.

WHEN YOU ARE ON THE RECEIVING END OF HONESTY

It's hard for us to have an honest conversation with a friend. It's even harder to be on the receiving end of someone else's honesty. Nobody likes to hear a friend communicate that you've hurt her or the relationship in some way. However, the *way* we receive feedback can make or break a relationship. Our attitude makes all the difference. Keeping that in mind, there are four "Be Attitudes" for responding well:

Be safe. You want to make it safe for her to be honest with you. Resist the urge to defend yourself. Seek to understand her perspective. Reflect back to her what you've heard—"What I hear you saying is . . . " Urge her on with phrases like "This is important. I want to understand," or "Tell me more." Your initial goal is to make sure your friend feels heard.

The way we receive feedback can make or break a relationship.

Be accepting. Accept responsibility for what you can. Once you've heard well, clear up any misunderstanding, if there is any. Pray as you're listening and interacting, asking God to help you handle this conversation well.

Be apologetic. Apologize without a "but." Even if you feel she has some responsibility, own the part that's yours. Offer a full apology that not only expresses that you're sorry, it includes what you're sorry about, and it asks for forgiveness.

Be appreciative. Thank her for her courage. Affirm her for caring enough to communicate her concern. Encourage her to always bring concerns to you as soon as they appear.

THE FOUNDATION OF FORGIVENESS AND GRACE

Theologian Paul Wadell said, "Friendships cannot last unless the friends become skilled in justice, generosity, and patience. They have no future without the virtues of loyalty, trustworthiness, care, and forgiveness." If you and I spend any amount of time with another imperfect human being, we'll need to have some way to handle disappointments along the way. Ephesians 4:32 gives us direction on what to do: "Be kind to one another, tenderhearted, forgiving one another, as God in Christ forgave you."

Honesty is important. Being a person someone can be honest with is valuable. However, it's forgiveness and grace that serve as a firm foundation for friendship. These beautiful gifts, given to us first by God, allow us to handle the little irritations that happen in every friendship.

John Swinton addressed this when he said, "Friendship is the place where forgiveness begins. The simplest slights can become unforgivable if we don't practice forgiveness regularly." Forgiveness allows you to keep your heart uncluttered and available to God. It keeps your attitude positive. It even prepares the way for you to have critical conversations, when necessary.

Grace allows another person to be human. To make mistakes. To get a pass when life is hard. To be loved when we're not at our best. Grace releases a friend from the expectation of perfection. We can give grace because Christ first gave it to us. We're reminded of this in John 1:16, "For from his fullness we all have received, grace upon grace."

What's the difference between forgiveness and grace? Forgiveness is specific; grace is all-encompassing. Forgiveness is a decision. Grace is an attitude. Forgiveness brings healing. Grace brings hope.

Sometimes forgiveness and grace are all we need to handle friendship frustrations. Sometimes they're the first steps we take before we address a friendship foul. At all times, they are the foundation of truly being better together.

FROM ANNE'S HEART

Reading about my mom's friendship breakup brought back emotions that I thought had been dealt with long ago. You see, I was on the receiving end of my own "We can no longer be friends" speech. It had been a toxic relationship so this conversation was bound to happen. I just didn't imagine I would be the one hearing those words. I sat there silently listening to all of the problems she had with me. Things I had confided in her over the years suddenly became ammunition.

All too often we approach conflict resolution like an old Western shootout. Both people have their guns locked and loaded—it's only a matter of who fires the fastest. Emotions run high in these situations. This is how I used to approach it until another friendship situation that happened in high school.

It was my senior year and I was having friendship problems. I was feeling left out of a friendship circle that included my brother. Looking back, it seems petty, but it's a hard thing to swallow when your friends start asking your little brother to hang out but not you.

> As our dessert was arriving, she sincerely said to me, "Anne, I just wanted to tell you I am so sorry for the way I treated you in high school."

One friendship in particular was the most difficult. I asked her to meet me for coffee to talk through it. In the hours before our meeting, I was a nervous wreck. My dad encouraged me to write down what I wanted to talk about. He then shared a picture that has stuck with me all these years.

Anytime you have conflict and someone begins sharing their frustrations, imagine they are physically laying each thing on a table between the two of you. It is then your responsibility to pick up and own what is yours and leave the rest on the table. Just because your friend has laid out something doesn't mean you have to carry it.

While my high school friend and I came to a mutual understanding, I never felt like it was the same again. We drifted apart after that. Last year, I found myself in the same city she now lived in and I decided to reach out to her. We sat across from each other at dinner, sharing what had transpired in our lives over the past twelve years. As our dessert was arriving, she sincerely said to me, "Anne, I just wanted to tell you that I am so sorry for how I treated you in high school." Twelve years after my initial conversation with her was when I heard those healing words. Twelve years, girls! Gratefully, I said thank you and I offered my forgiveness. We still don't talk all that much, but I no longer have the lens of hurt when I think of her.

When someone has caused us pain, often our first instinct is to hold on to that pain because we want justice. But what if I had never heard "I am sorry"? What if there was never any mutual resolution to the pain? What if I had carried everything that was laid out on the table for the last twelve years? I can't imagine the bitterness that would be in my heart.

My mom often says that forgiveness is letting someone off our hook and putting them on God's hook. We can only put them on God's hook when we fully give it to Him. Even though my breakup friend hasn't shown up in my life physically, just thinking about it all these years later weighs me down with revisited hurt, betrayal, and sadness. As I am writing this out, I feel another one of those moments where God taps me on the shoulder and gently says, "Give her to Me." This time around, I am gladly taking it off and handing it to Him. He can be the One to deal with the emotions. He can be the One to give justice. I can continue to live life in freedom. So can you.

SOMETHING TO THINK ABOUT:
What friendship hurt are you still carrying with you? What did you pick up that you shouldn't be carrying? What do you need to give to God so you can experience freedom?

Today's Friendship Assignment

Evaluate your friendships. Are there any that are naturally fading? Is that okay with you?

Do you have any friendship fiascos you need to tend to?

How are you doing with forgiveness and grace?

## CHAPTER 10

Encouraging Together
"You've got this! You can do it!"

L et's face it, your two-year-old isn't likely to walk up to you and say, "Gee, Mom, you're doing a great job!" And if you have a teenager, you won't be hearing encouraging words for quite a few years. After all, they are way smarter than you are (cough cough)! Even if you have an appreciative, attentive husband, it's likely his positive words don't have quite the same feel as hearing a sincere "Atta girl" from a gal pal who understands your life!

Motherhood is a thankless job. You don't feel a true "sense of accomplishment" for a whole lot of years. One season melts into the next season without taking the time to celebrate what you actually finished (think about it—when has anyone ever thrown you a "You Successfully Potty-Trained Your Toddler" party?). We desperately need some girlfriends who cheer for us along the marathon of motherhood.

Unfortunately, we're far better at tearing each other down than lifting each other up. Without even realizing it, the enemy twists our opinions and preferences into some form of counterfeit truth, causing us to believe that if a mom doesn't do things the "right" way (our way), she's wrong, "less than," or misguided in some way. We believe so strongly in whatever we believe in (breastfeeding, co-sleeping, organic eating, staying home, going to work, using cloth diapers . . . the list goes on and on!), that we easily forget another mom might have a different viewpoint than we have. In order for us to be truly better together, mom jeers need to be turned into mom cheers.

CHANGING THE STORY

Our granddaughter Marie was almost nine weeks premature. Erica planned to breastfeed Marie, so she instructed the nurses in the NICU not to give Marie a bottle. She began pumping breast milk right away because Marie was too small initially to even latch on and was nourished through a nasogastric tube. When the doctor gave the go-ahead to remove the NG tube and begin feeding her normally, she had a lot of issues latching on. Eventually Erica discovered that, against her wishes, the hospital was giving Marie bottles rather than waiting for Erica to arrive.

It became evident that Marie preferred the bottle to nursing. It was just easier for her. Erica worked with a lactation consultant through the hospital. She used a breast shield to try to help Marie latch on. She rented a high-quality breast pump through the hospital to keep up her milk supply. She drank milk thistle tea to help with milk production. She began attending the local La Leche League.

Even though Erica connected with a consultant through La Leche League, when I arrived a few weeks after Marie came home, mom and baby were still struggling with breastfeeding. As one who nursed all four of my biological kids, I pulled out every trick in the book, including tapping into the wisdom of a friend who is a lactation consultant. We threw Erica's determination, my experience, the best "tools" available, the encouragement of her local breastfeeding community, and the wisdom of three different lactation consultants at it and it just wasn't working. Finally Erica said in exhaustion, "I just can't do this anymore." She hung up breastfeeding for good and decided to be grateful for formula.

Any pro-breastfeeding mom seeing Erica give Marie a bottle would have no knowledge of that difficult journey. She would have no way of knowing how hard Erica tried to make breastfeeding work. However, it's entirely possible someone judged her somewhere along the way.

We were part of a moms group and she was going through infertility issues. I had already had my share of them, so I shared my experiences with her. We started talking more and more. One summer our families decided to go on vacation together. We figured if we could handle that, we must have something special. Eight years and eight vacations later, we're still best friends and our families are as close as families can get. We even live down the street from each other. —TERI

Every decision a mom makes takes into consideration her beliefs, experiences, desires, circumstances, and knowledge. Neither you nor I know the full scope of her reality. We have to remember this when judgment creeps in and we want to think critical thoughts. We have to change the story we tell ourselves, knock off the judgment, and be cheerleaders instead of opponents. We're all united and on the same team. We have to look for opportunities to cheer our teammates. After all, we're all in this together!

Team Mom is filled with women who are tired, discouraged, and even disillusioned at times. Some are sleep deprived. Most are craving "just a few minutes to myself." They're desperate to know they're making a difference, but most days wonder if they really are. The mom guilt is weighing them down. They are run ragged with responsibility, overwhelmed with laundry, and dishes, and meal-making, and keeping up with the house.

You and I can make a difference. Even with something as small as a smile.

HIGH-FIVE WITH YOUR EYES

It's a letter I'll never forgot from a mom I may personally never know:

Dear Jill, several weeks ago, you and I crossed paths at Walmart. I was trying to pick up a few things with my kids in tow. They were tired and weren't handling the shopping excursion well at all. I was battling both of them when you came around the corner, pushing your cart. You saw me. Then you smiled at me with a smile that simply said, "I understand. Hang in there, girlfriend." Suddenly I had the strength of two moms! I knew I could finish this shopping trip and make it home. I knew I could "be the mom" and lead my kids through this!

I know it's probably not often you get to encourage another mom in the men's underwear department of Walmart without saying a single word. But you did that day and I wanted you to know.

Wow! What a powerful letter! Believe it or not, I actually remember seeing her. I remember having compassion and thinking *Been there, done that*. I want to call attention to three particular statements she made:

• **You saw me.** I'll admit I'm not always the best at noticing people. I'm not particularly observant. Often in my own little "introvert" world, I can easily look through someone without even realizing it. But that day, I saw her, and it communicated value to her.

• **You smiled at me.** Too often we underestimate the power of a small gesture. Something as simple as a smile takes very little effort on our part but can make a huge difference in someone's life! It's like giving them a high five with your eyes!

• **Suddenly I had the strength of two moms.** That's what encouragement does. It gives us courage. Boosts our batteries. Refreshes our weary souls. It's a gift we can give another mom and it doesn't cost a dime!

What are some ways you can encourage any mom you see whether you know her or not? In addition to an understanding smile, you can:

1) Hold the door open so she can navigate her stroller through— she'll be grateful she won't have to stretch.

2) Pick up the blanket her toddler threw on the floor at the grocery store . . . she'll be thankful for the break because she's already picked it up a dozen times in the last ten minutes.

3) Carry drinks or her tray to the table in a restaurant. She'll be grateful she doesn't have to make several trips back and forth.

4) Play peek-a-boo with her son at the restaurant so she can actually eat a few bites uninterrupted.

5) Walk with her fussy infant on an airplane, letting her know that you've been in her shoes before.

6) Compliment her on her kids, no matter how old they are. She needs to hear it.

In the book of Hebrews we are told to "encourage one another daily" (3:13a NIV). Encouragement is the fuel that keeps us motivated as moms. Here are some ways you can encourage a bosom buddy:

1) *Be the friend you wish you had.* Matthew 6:12 reminds us to "do for others what you would like them to do for you." Be thoughtful, caring, and engaged. These are character traits most of us long for in a friend.

2. *Surprise her with little gifts in the mail or dropped off on her porch.* Unexpected, for no reason, "thinking of you" gifts bring so much encouragement! You can also surprise a friend with something you know they need. My friend Pam, who lives two thousand miles away, saw me ask on Facebook what kind of lip balm people found helpful. I'd had chapped lips for months! Three days later a little package of Pam's favorite brand of lip balm arrived in my mailbox! What a thoughtful surprise!

3) *Affirm the little things.* Because you tend to be in each other's world, watch for the little things she does that no one probably sees. Notice and affirm them. Anne and Matt recently had their friend Aimee come to visit with her two girls. Toward the end of the weekend, Aimee said to Anne, "Your house is filled with Jesus. I love that you don't care about having a perfect house." What an encouragement to Anne when she struggles with her outiness.

4) *Speak words of life to her.* Romans 1:12 reminds us that we are "mutually encouraged by each other's faith." Proverbs 12:25 (NIV)declares, "Anxiety weighs down the heart, but a kind word cheers it up." Sometimes a friend just needs to hear you say, "You can do this!" Sometimes she needs to be reminded of God's truth to infuse light into a dark moment.

5) *Help her fold laundry.* Or do dishes. Or bake cookies. When we help one another out with the daily tasks of motherhood, it's an encouraging act of love. My friend Sue, who has older kids, runs errands with her friend Jody, who has younger kids. Sue and Jody enjoy the talk time in the car and then Sue stays in the car with Jody's kids so she doesn't have to drag them in and out of several stores. What a gift of encouragement this is to Jody!

This world does a fine job tearing people down. You and I have some important work to do building each other up. As we say at Hearts at Home: When we invest in a mom, we influence a family, improve a community, and impact the world!

ME TOO!

I invited a mom I didn't know well to join us for lunch after Mom2Mom one day. We walked into my house and the first thing I saw were the breakfast dishes on the table. I cringed. The first thing she saw were the breakfast dishes on the table. She smiled and said, "You have no idea how much I needed to see this."

Letting another mom peek into your imperfect life can be some of the best encouragement you can offer. When she sees your laundry piled up, she thinks, *I'm normal.* When she witnesses your two-year-old having a meltdown at church or overhears your teenager respond to you with a little too much sass, she thinks, *My kids are normal.* Our "I was mortified" situation is often another mom's "I was encouraged" situation. We all need "me too" moments with other moms.

When you have the opportunity, share your struggles openly. Your honesty will likely validate feelings she's had but maybe not expressed. Share your successes as well. Sometimes knowing there's light at the end of the tunnel is just the encouragement another mom needs to keep on keepin' on.

LIVE. LOVE. LAUGH. AND THEN LAUGH SOME MORE.

My husband picked up two pink plastic flamingos at a garage sale and proudly placed them around the little pond in our yard. He thought they looked good, and I thought they looked tacky. My friend Becky was visiting one day and she asked about the pink flamingos. I told her that Mark and I had very different opinions about them. I didn't notice that she put them in her car when she left.

A couple days later, we went to Dave and Becky's house for dinner. Our two pink flamingos were proudly displayed in her yard. As we left, Mark grabbed the birds and put them in our car. Once we got home, we decided to have some more fun with this. We typed a ransom note for "their" pink flamingos and dropped it in the mail!

When was the last time you played with a friend? You know . . . when you did something silly or "just because"? When you laughed until you nearly peed your pants? When you went out for coffee with a friend and stayed so late laughing and sharing stories that the restaurant had to tell you they were closing and you had to go home? How about when you gathered a group of gals for a night of Bunco? Sometimes a girl just wants to have fun!

When I ask moms what their favorite parts of a Hearts at Home conference weekend are, they usually share about their favorite speaker, the workshop(s) that impacted them the most, and how much they loved their time laughing together in a hotel room with other moms. The conference trip gives moms permission to play together. Even if you have to drive eight or ten hours to get to a conference, if you put three or four moms in a car, an eight-hour road trip will only feel like a couple hours! You'll laugh, tell stories, and have many "me too" moments.

> *This world does a fine job tearing people down. You and I have some important work to do building each other up.*

What if we did that more often than once a year? What if we occasionally called up a girlfriend and asked her to go somewhere for twenty-four hours? What if we hosted a once-a-month Bunco girls night out? What if we organized a slumber party for our moms group, the moms in the neighborhood, or the girls in our small group at church? I know—it's not easy to do. There's childcare to arrange, and extracting a mom from her daily mom duties is challenging. But these MOMents are the kind of encouragement we desperately need! They gather the tribe, let mom enjoy a little time off, and bring refreshment to our weary souls. You and I can't afford not to do it!

IT'S [NOT] THE THOUGHT THAT COUNTS

Anne recently issued the following challenge on her blog, and it belongs right here on these closing pages about encouraging one another. May this motivate us from thought to action: "Do you ever have those moments where someone pops into your head randomly? Or you know a friend who is struggling and you continually think about and, if you're a person of faith, pray for them? Here's the thing . . .

How do they know they've been thought of?

How do they know they've been prayed for?

Life's struggles are often accompanied by loneliness, discouragement, and/or anxiety. We aren't meant to carry these loads alone. We are built for relationship. Yet, in the midst of trials, it is often the last thing on our minds to seek out friendship and encouragement.

We aren't meant to carry life's struggles alone. So this is what I've come to realize: It's *not* the thought that counts.

There have been numerous times when people will randomly come to mind or I just can't stop thinking about them. I've begun to recognize, many times, this is God laying them on my heart for the purpose of praying for or encouraging them. Therefore, it's a call to action.

Relationships can be hard, especially for an introvert, like myself, who values in-depth friendships. Because of this, I find it doesn't come naturally to casually "check in" on someone or let them know I'm thinking about them. I know some people who are incredibly gifted with this skill in relationships. And this is what I've come to identify: It *is* a skill, and skills can be mastered with practice.

My neighbor is a wonderful example of someone who utilizes this skill well. On several occasions, she has brought by little gifts for the kids or overstock from her pantry. To me, it says, *"I was thinking about you."*

She'll never know . . . unless you tell her.

When my dad experienced a midlife crisis and left for three months, the outpouring of love I experienced was incredible. And while I may not have responded to every single message or text, the fact that someone took a moment to let me know they were thinking about me was appreciated. I felt like I had a community around me . . . that I wasn't alone.

So, I am challenging myself to intentionally exercise this skill. How about you?

The next time you interact with a young mom and think, *She's a good mom!*—**tell her.**

The next time you are baking cookies and think *I should double this recipe and take some to the neighbors*—**go for it.**

The next time you can't get an old friend off your mind— **let her know.**

The next time you see someone with fabulous hair— **be bold and tell her!**

The next time a friend going through a difficult time comes to mind—**pray for her and let her know.**

The next time you think *I would love to do coffee with her*— **text her and make a date.**

You never know what that person is going through or experiencing in that moment. Your text or quick encouragement may be exactly what they need. **And she'll never know . . . unless you tell her."**[1]

WE ARE BETTER TOGETHER

We've come a long way on the pages of this book. We started our journey laying the foundation of why friendship matters. We established we're designed for community. We talked about the stages of friendship, including MBFs (Might Be Friends), TBFs (Trying to Be Friends), GGFs (Good Girlfriends), and BFFs (I think we all know what a BFF is!).

We've explored how personalities and temperaments affect friendship. We've identified the friendship frame that establishes these levels of friendships: dear friends, cheer friends, peer friends, and sphere friends. We've spent the remainder of our time exploring how to practically do this mom thing together.

It's time now for us to make a commitment. Anne and I invite you to join us in the Better Together Commitment.

THE BETTER TOGETHER COMMITMENT

Understanding I can do this mom thing better with other moms in my life, I will do my best to:

Stop trying to do life alone.

Find the courage to strike up conversations.

Keep the circle broken, always making room for another mom.

Move from passively waiting to actively pursuing friendship.

Stop judging and start accepting moms who are different from me.

Resist the urge to compare my insides to another mom's outsides.

Remember that I have strengths other moms can benefit from.

Stop offering to help and start helping.

Be Jesus to those around me.

Share my story so another mom can walk through her story.

Pray with and for my friends.

Remember my value is in Christ alone.

Practice forgiveness.

Let another mom peek into my imperfect life.

Encourage other moms whenever I can.

Share with another mom that we are all better together.

You have so much to offer the women God has put around you. Your life is designed to intersect with other moms' lives. God longs to connect the dots in ways that only He can. May you and I step deeper into the world of mom friendships and discover all the ways we really are better together.

NEXT STEPS FOR YOUR BETTER TOGETHER JOURNEY:

Find more Better Together Resources at
www.bettertogetherbook.com

Get monthly encouragement from Hearts at Home! Sign up for our
free Hearts On-The-Go E-Newsletter at www.HeartsatHome.org.

Attend a Hearts at Home Conference! If there's not a conference near
you, you can order a Conference To-Go and share it with a friend.

Stay in touch with Anne and me through our blogs:
www.JillSavage.org and www.EverydaySmallThings.com

Visit the No More Perfect website: www.NoMorePerfect.com.
You'll find free videos and resources to continue your journey.

Like the "Hearts at Home" Facebook Page.
You'll join an online community of moms who are
virtually doing life together!

NOTES

Chapter 1—Where It All Begins

1. Beth Azar, "A new stress paradigm for women," *Monitor on Psychology* 31, no. 7 (July/August 2000): 12.
2. S. E. Taylor, L. C. Klein, B. P. Lewis, T. L. Gruenewald, R. A. R. Gurung, and J. A. Updegraff, "Biobehavioral Responses to Stress in Females: Tend-and-Befriend, Not Fight-or-Flight," *Psychol Rev* 107, no. 3 (July 2000): 411–29.
3. Gale Berkowitz, "UCLA Study on Friendship among Women: An alternative to fight or flight," n.p., 2002, http://robotics.usc.edu/~agents/miscellaneous/resources/data/UCLA_Study_On_Friendship_Among_Women.pdf.

Chapter 2—Who Are You "Momming" With?

1. Karen Ehman, *A Life That Says Welcome: Simple Ways to Open Your Heart & Home to Others* (Grand Rapids, Revell, 2006), 18.
2. Sara Horn, "Keep Your Circle Broken: When It's Hard Making Friends," Perfectly Imperfect (blog), July 6, 2015, http://www.sarahorn.com/2015/07/06/hard-making-friends/.

Chapter 3—Variety Is the Spice of Life!

1. Wikipedia contributors, "Keeping up with the Joneses," Wikipedia, The Free Encyclopedia, https://en.wikipedia.org/wiki/Keeping_up_with_the_Joneses.
2. Lori Neff, "Inside 'The End', Part 3," Lori Neff (blog), October 19, 2015, http://lorineff.com/2015/10/04/inside-the-end-part-3/.

Chapter 5—Helping Together

1. Tessa Afshar, "Foot Washing," Tessa Afshar (blog), August 25, 2013, http://www.tessaafshar.com/blog/foot-washing/.

Chapter 6—Caring Together

1. Julie Jordan, "Sandra Bullock Puts Rumors to Rest about Having More Kids," *People*, April 23, 2015, http://www.people.com/people/package/article/0,,20913899_20917464,00.html.

Chapter 10—Encouraging Together

1. Anne McClane, "It's (Not) the Thought That Counts," Everyday Small Things (blog), August 14, 2015, http://everydaysmallthings.com/its-not-the-thought-that-counts/.

TBF (TRYING TO BE FRIENDS) CONVERSATION STARTERS

Tell me about your family.

How old are your kids and what is one thing each kid has taught you?

Where did you grow up?

Tell me your story (your life story, your faith story, whatever story she'd like to share . . .).

Do you have any siblings?

Does your extended family live nearby?

What does your family do on the weekends?

What do you like to do in your spare time?

Do you have any hobbies?

Did you go to college? If so, where? What did you study?

What about motherhood has surprised you?

Does your family ever play board games? Do you have a favorite?

Do you have any pets? Are you more of a cat or a dog person?

Do you drink coffee or tea?

Do you have a favorite holiday?

What did you do last weekend?

What do you like to do to relax?

Are you refueled by being alone or by being with people?

Got any advice you'd share with a new mom?

Did you have a favorite subject in school?

Did you have a least favorite subject in school?

What activities were you involved in, in high school?

If you're comfortable, I'd love to hear about the family you grew up in.

What did/do your parents do?

Are you a country girl or a city girl?

Where do you see yourself five years from now?

What did you do BK (before kids)?

What was your least favorite job you've ever had?

Does your family take a summer vacation? Where do you go?

Does your family have any birthday traditions?

Have you ever been outside of the country? If so, where?

What's your favorite activity to do with your kids on a rainy day?

How do you feel about cooking? Like it? Dislike it?

Does anyone in your family have any food allergies?

Do you have a favorite food? Favorite dessert?

Do you have a favorite restaurant?

Have you ever done freezer cooking?

Have you seen a movie lately? If so, what was it and would you recommend it?

Are you reading anything right now? Would you recommend it?

What's the best mothering book you've read?

What's the best marriage book you've read?

Have you and your husband ever gone on a marriage retreat?

Are you involved in a church?

Do you have a favorite season of the year? What do you like most about it?

Do you have any television shows you watch on a regular basis?

What is the best parenting advice you've received?

What's the best marriage advice you've received?

Do you have any goals for yourself?

Do you have any plans for next weekend?

What's for dinner tonight?

Do you make a plan for dinner or wait till five and start thinking about it?

What have you done for fun lately?

For moms of littles: Do you have any potty-training or teething tips?

For moms of teens: What's one thing you would tell a mom who's just starting the teen years?

Do you have a cleaning routine?

Do you have a dentist/doctor/pediatrician/eye doctor you love?

Got any tips for organizing for the house?

Do you have a bedtime routine with your kids? How do you do it?

When was your last date night? What did you do?

When was the last time you went away for an overnight with your husband?

Do you have any tips for back to school?

Do you have a favorite park you like to take the kids to?

Are you crafty? What do you like to create?

Are you on Pinterest? What do you use it for?

What social media do you use? Facebook? Twitter? Pinterest? Instagram? Periscope?

Need more ideas on the go? Check out the "Questions In A Box" App!

MPI: Mothering Personality Inventory

This quiz provides you guidance for the chapter 3 discussion on mothering personalities.

For each trait that makes up our personality, there are some evaluating statements in groups of two. Read each statement and determine which best describes you in each group.

Once you have finished all of the evaluating questions, transfer your results to pages 215–217. Then plot where you are on the spectrum. For instance, if there are seven questions and you get four 1s and three 2s, you're going to be somewhere near the center of the spectrum, slightly left of center. If there are seven questions and you get one 1 and six 2s, you'll plot yourself to the far right of the spectrum. Understanding where you are on the spectrum helps you to understand if that is a strong personality trait or a less pronounced personality trait.

You can take one trait evaluation at a time and hop back over to chapter 3 to read about that trait and how it affects your relationships, or you can take the whole evaluation at once and then go back and read about all of your personality traits and how they affect your friendships.

Evaluating Statements for Personality Trait #1:
(These have to do with how you are emotionally refueled.)

1) I prefer one-on-one conversations.
2) I prefer group conversations.

1) I prefer texting conversations.
2) I prefer talking on the phone or in person.

1) I enjoy solitude.
2) I love a great party.

1) I enjoy work that allows me to dive in with few interruptions.
2) I love activity, and working in a group environment.

1) I like to celebrate birthdays on a small scale with just a few family and friends.
2) It's a birthday . . . let's party!

1) I have one hobby.
2) I enjoy several hobbies.

1) I am refueled by being alone.
2) I am refueled by being with people.

# of 1s _____ # of 2s _____

Evaluating Statements for Personality Trait #2:
(These have to do with how you process information.)

1) When I'm trying to figure something out, I think about all the options.
2) When I'm trying to figure something out, I need to process with someone.

1) I think, think, and think some more.
2) I talk, and talk, and talk some more.

1) I sometimes forget to let my spouse know that I'm thinking about something.
2) My spouse always knows what I'm thinking about!

1) In a group setting, I'm not likely to jump in and start the discussion.
2) In a group setting, I'm likely to be the one to share my thoughts first.

1) I tend to organize what I'm going to say before I say it.
2) I start speaking and let the words take their course.

1) If I have a need, I keep it to myself and try to come up with my own solutions.
2) If I have a need, I call and ask someone to help me think through it.

1) Sometimes I forget to tell others the details of an activity.
2) Sometimes others get annoyed at how much information I share with them.

# of 1s _____ # of 2s _____

Evaluating Statements for Personality Trait #3:
(These have to do with how you organize things.)

1) I'm a filer, not a piler.
2) I'm more often a piler than a filer.

1) I have one "to-do" list that keeps me organized.
2) I use sticky notes for everything.

1) I love the peacefulness of order.
2) I enjoy and am comfortable with an imperfect messy home environment.

1) I know where things are. I don't have to see them to remember them.
2) If I don't see something, I might forget about it. (Out of sight, out of mind.)

1) I love having as close to nothing on my kitchen counters as I can.
2) I have a lot of stuff on my kitchen counters.

1) Everything has a home—you just put things in their home.
2) Sometimes I don't know what to do with all my kids' stuff.

1) I love to store things in bins with clear labels on the outside.
2) I have an "everything drawer" that I sort through to find what I'm looking for.

# of 1s _____ # of 2s _____

Evaluating Statements for Personality Trait #4:
(These have to do with how you manage your time.)

1) I hardly use a calendar.
2) I can't live without my calendar!

1) I often don't have a plan for the day. I wait to see how I'm feeling.
2) I have a plan for tomorrow already in my head.

1) If someone makes a suggestion to do something, I might jump at the opportunity.
2) If someone makes a suggestion to do something, I might have trouble making the change in my mind.

1) Too often I go to the store and forget something I needed because my list is a bit disorganized and might be on the back of a napkin.
2) I occasionally forget something I need at the store, but not very often because I have a very detailed list I use as I shop.

1) I'd love to take my child to story hour at the library, but I keep forgetting when it is.
2) We go to story hour at the library every week.

1) Spontaneity and I are like chocolate and peanut butter.
2) Spontaneity and I are like oil and water.

# of 1s _____ # of 2s _____

Evaluating Statements for Personality Trait #5:
(These have to do with your physical and emotional capacity.)

1) I prefer to keep my schedule simple and manageable.
2) My calendar is full—maybe too full at times.

1) I so wish I had more energy.
2) I'm rarely low on energy.

1) I can only focus on and handle a few things at a time.
2) I can juggle many thing and multitask easily.

1) I'm careful about how much I say yes to because I know my limits.
2) It sometimes feels like I'm doing more of the work at home or in a group than others.

1) I love doing nothing on occasion.
2) There's always something that needs to be done.

1) I love to listen to my kids.
2) I love to help my kids do something.

1) I struggle with thinking I should be doing so much more.
2) I forget to slow down and just hang out with the family without an agenda.

# of 1s _____ # of 2s _____

Personality Trait #1

of 1s _____ # of 2s _____

More 1s—you're probably more of an Introvert.
More 2s—you're probably more of an Extrovert.

So where are you on the Spectrum? Draw a line and plot where you are.

INTROVERTED   **EXTROVERTED**

MORE 1s ◄————————————————————► MORE 2s

Personality Trait #2

of 1s _____ # of 2s _____

If you have more 1s, you are likely an Internal Processing Person.
If you have more 2s, you are likely an External Processing Person.

So where are you on the Spectrum? Draw a line and plot where you are.

INTERNAL PROCESSOR   **EXTERNAL PROCESSOR**

MORE 1s ◄————————————————————► MORE 2s

Personality Trait #3

of 1s _____ # of 2s _____

If you have more 1s, when it comes to home organization,
you are an Innie.

If you have more 2s, when it comes to home organization,
you are an Outie.

So where are you on the Spectrum? Draw a line and plot where you are.

Personality Trait #4

of 1s _____ # of 2s _____

If you have more 1s, you're likely a Spontaneous Mom.
If you have more 2s, you're likely a Structured Mom.

So where are you on the Spectrum? Draw a line and plot where you are.

Personality Trait #5

\# of 1s _____ \# of 2s _____

If you have more 1s, you are likely a Medium-Low Capacity Person.
If you have more 2s, you are likely a Medium-High Capacity Person.

So where are you on the Spectrum? Draw a line and plot where you are.

MEDIUM-LOW CAPACITY — MORE 1s ◄───────────► MORE 2s — **MEDIUM-HIGH CAPACITY**

"I praise you because I am fearfully and wonderfully made."
Psalm 139:14 NIV

Appendix C

BETTER TOGETHER MOM CO-OPS
Better Together Once-a-Month Cooking

The secret to successful once-a-month cooking is the planning. Here are nine steps to cook for a day and eat for a month.

1) *Ask a friend to join you.* The goal is not only to make dinnertime easier but also to do life together with a friend. When considering who to ask, think about family size and food preferences. Don't forget to think about possible food allergies. Once you decide on your cooking partner, decide whose kitchen you'll use. Does one kitchen have more counter space or are they similar and you can alternate monthly? Is one house better for cooking and the other for childcare? If your church has a large kitchen, that might be an option to consider, as well.

2) *Plan a day.* Choose a day when someone else (dad, grandma, another friend) can watch the kids in a location away from where the cooking is taking place. Some friends I know work out a deal with their husbands. The two friends cook together monthly on a Saturday. One month, dad #1 watches all the kids and dad #2 helps the moms by washing dishes throughout the prep day (there's a lot of dishwashing!). The next month the dads trade places.

3) *Plan your meals.* Sit down with your friend and list out your family's favorite meals that can be frozen. Determine how many meals you'll actually make. Fifteen to twenty meals for each family is probably the most you should attempt for a day. If you do twenty meals for each family, you actually only need ten different recipes, assuming your family doesn't

219

mind the same meal twice within a month. You'll then make four batches of each recipe.

4) *Modify your recipes.* To determine the quantity of the ingredients you will need to buy, quadruple every recipe you'll be making.

5) *Make your shopping list.* Based upon your quadrupled computations, make your shopping list. Agree with your cooking partner on the types of ingredients you'll use: Organic or not? No-antibiotic meat or not? Brand preferences? Don't forgot freezer bags and aluminum foil (if you're making casseroles in pans). If you'd like to have the option of taking a freezer meal to someone who's sick or just had a baby, you might want to pick up some disposable pans, as well. Tip: Your local dollar store is a great place to pick up disposable pans. They are often packaged in groups of three! Three disposable casserole pans for $1!

6) *Shop.* Decide how you will shop. Some cooking duos do the shopping together. Others alternate shopping responsibilities monthly. Decide also where you'll shop.

7) *Cook.* The day has arrived! Turn on some music and enjoy this time with your friend. Before you start cooking, you'll want to label your freezer bags with the name of the meal and cooking directions. Make sure you've thought ahead about what you'll do for lunch for the two of you and for your families for dinner. This might be a good night for ordering pizza after such a big day of cooking!

8) *Freeze.* If you freeze in freezer bags, you'll want to get as much air out of the bags as possible. If you have limited freezer space, you can freeze the meals flat on a cookie sheet or directly on the freezer shelf until they

reach their frozen shape. This will keep them from accidentally freezing together. Then stack the frozen meals in your freezer. Meat loaf can be frozen in one of two ways:

1) Form it into the loaf to determine the size you want. Then flatten the loaf and freeze it flat in a freezer bag. Once thawed, you can form it into its loaf form and pop it in the oven. This option actually thaws faster because the meat is only about an inch thick.

2) Make it into its loaf shape, wrap it in plastic wrap and then aluminum foil. Label the foil wrap and pop it in the freezer.

Tip: When making a meal to be frozen then cooked in the Crock-pot, it's better to freeze it upright than flat. Flat items stack better in the freezer, but a flat frozen meal won't fit into a Crock-pot. Hold the bag by the ziplock closure and set the meal in the freezer upright; then, it should fit nicely in the bottom of the Crock-pot without the added step of needing to thaw it some first.

9) *Enjoy!* Some meals can go straight from the freezer to the Crock-pot. Others need to be moved from the freezer to the refrigerator to thaw.

BETTER TOGETHER FREEZER MEAL CO-OP

The Freezer Meal Co-op requires less prep work but involves more people. Here are six steps to organize a successful meal exchange:

1) *Invite five to eight moms to join you in your freezer meal exchange.* You'll want to consider family size, food preferences, and cooking styles (if your family primarily eats the Paleo diet, you'll want to find other families who

are eating the same way!). Families with food allergies may want to find other families with similar allergies.

2) *Determine how often you want to trade.* Some groups do it monthly, others every six weeks, and still others shoot for every other month. You'll end up with the same number of meals as moms in your group. (If you have six moms, you'll have six meals at your exchange.)

3) *Meet together to plan meals.* You'll want to discuss food likes and dis-likes. Considering this information, have each person determine what meal they will provide for the swap. Marinated meats, casseroles, soups, stews, lasagna, and meat loaf make great freezer meals. Remember you are each only making one recipe, but you are making that one recipe for each member of the co-op. If one of your members doesn't like a certain ingredient, like onions, you can choose to leave that ingredient out of their meal or choose another meal for your exchange that doesn't have any disliked ingredients. When you meet to plan meals, you'll also want to set your exchange date and location.

4) *Choose your cooking day.* Since you're exchanging freezer meals, it's fine to already have the meals frozen if you have the freezer space to hold them. If freezer space allows, you might want to cook a couple of days ahead of the exchange date. This way if you end up with a sick kid on cooking day, you've got an extra day or two to fall back on.

5) *Meet, exchange, and plan the next month.* Decide who will host the ex-change or select a place (like a restaurant or church) to meet. Each co-op member brings her meals in a cooler. Lay out all the meals on a table or kitchen counter and then have each member take one of each recipe to put in her cooler. If you choose to meet in a public place like a restaurant,

you can all park near one another and exchange them in the parking lot! Head home and pop your meals in your freezer. (Hop over to jillsavage. org to download your free freezer meal log to post on your refrigerator!)

6) *Evaluate recipes after each exchange.* Remind everyone that the reason you evaluate is to make sure the recipes being made are a good fit for the group. It's important to state right up front that we need to keep egos out of this. Need more help? Check out www.30daygourmet.com.

BETTER TOGETHER CHRISTMAS COOKIE BAKING DAY

Baking with another mom allows you to accomplish two things at once: investing in a relationship and investing in your family (my family LOVES it when I bake!). Here are the steps to make a fun-filled day of baking happen:

1) *Invite a friend.* This could be a day to invest in a GGF (Good Girlfriend) relationship or it could even be a TBF (Trying To Be Friends) activity.

2) *Select a day.* Depending on the ages of your kids, you'll need to decide if this is best done without kids or if the kids will play well (and eat some of your work!) while you are kitchen focused.

3) *Select the recipes you'll tackle.* Two to six different recipes are probably the most you should tackle in a day. You'll likely be doubling or quadrupling each recipe, especially if you're wanting to share the treats, give them as gifts, or freeze them.

4) *Create a shopping list.* Calculate the amount of ingredients you'll need. Depending on whether you're doubling or quadrupling the recipes, you'll need to do the math.

5) *Shop.* Shop with your friend or decide that the person whose kitchen will not be used will be the shopper. Split the cost of the ingredients.

6) *Bake.* Start with recipes that require that you refrigerate the dough. You can also overlap recipes like making fudge while batches of cookies are baking. Tip: Keep a sink of warm, soapy water ready for washing mixing bowls, spatulas, and your mixer beaters that you'll need to use for your next recipe. This will also help you stay on top of the mess.

7) *Divide the cookies.* Prepare them for freezing, giving, or taking to an upcoming Christmas party.

8) *Enjoy!* Bask in the task accomplished and the time spent with a friend! Enjoy the fruits of your labor throughout the entire holiday season!

BETTER TOGETHER HOME PROJECT CO-OP

Tackle your to-do list and spend time with some friends by setting up a Home Project Co-op. Here's how to make it happen:

1) *Invite friends to join you.* You can successfully co-op with one other friend (actually that makes it a "trade" but you get the idea) to three other friends. Create your list of invite possibilities. Because this requires a three-to-four month commitment (three months if there are three of you in the co-op, four months if there are four of you in the co-op), you'll want to ask friends who are dependable.

2) *Whip out your calendars.* Determine if you'll do two-, three-, or four-hour time commitments. Then set up a time for each person to be served.

You can determine to go in alphabetical order or set dates based upon the timing of a project. For instance, one mom may want help stripping wallpaper but she's not ready to do that next month and would prefer to be served in a couple of months.

3) *Let the group members know what project(s) they'll be tackling.* Have the hosting mom think through her list of supplies she'll need for her project(s). If there's something she doesn't have, have her check with the group members before purchasing a tool or supply. Part of the benefit of doing life together is having the opportunity to borrow. Communication will help the group members know what to wear and if they need to bring any tools.

4) *Work together.* You'll accomplish tasks in a matter of hours that would have taken one person days (or weeks or months!) to complete. Enjoy the time working side by side, experiencing a sense of accomplishment, and delighting in the beauty of friendship.

Tips:

- If a conflict comes up, reschedule the workday so everyone can be present.
- Schedule your work time in the morning or afternoon but not over mealtime.
- Whoever is being served should have some drinks and maybe a light snack available.
- Take breaks as needed. Remember the purpose is to not only accomplish a project or two but to also have fun together.

BETTER TOGETHER DATE NIGHT SWAP

Every couple needs time together without kids. A Date Night Swap is just what you need to make that happen. Here's how to get your swap started:

1) *Invite a family.* Brainstorm with your husband to think of some couples you know who have a similar family size, similar parenting style, and similar ages of kids. You're not looking for a perfect match (there's not another YOU!) but just looking for enough similarities to make a good match. Decide who you'll reach out to first to see if they would be interested.

2) *Determine your trade schedule.* Do you want to trade once a week so you each get two dates a month or do you want to trade every two weeks so you each get one date a month? You could also trade once a month, allowing you to each get a date once every other month. That's not really often enough for keeping your marriage healthy, but if it's more than you're doing now, it's an improvement!

3) *Give an out.* The only way a trade works is if it's a good match for both families. Determine to give the arrangement a couple of trades (at least twice at each family's house) and then evaluate. State right up front that no feelings will be hurt if either one of you feel it's not going well for your kids. If it's going well, keep on trading! If not, end your swap and try another couple on that list you came up with.

4) *Enjoy your "time for two."* Don't feel like you have to spend money for your Date Night Swap. Remember, your house is empty . . . think of the possibilities with no kids at home!

Tips:

1) Once your kids are accustomed to the trade, you can add a once- or twice-a-year overnight trade into the mix. This allows for some extended couple time on occasion!

2) Discuss how you prefer to have disobedience handled. Agree upon a way you'll manage it when you swap.

BETTER TOGETHER SITTING TRADES

Every mom needs some time to herself. Sometimes a trade with another mom is the best way to make that happen!

1) *Ask a friend.* Invite a friend to set up a regular trade with you. You both need some "me" time on a regular basis.

2) *Set up a schedule.* The key to making it happen is in the planning. Determine a time that works for both of you and stick with it!

3) *Agree on how to handle behavior issues.* It's best to talk about this right up front so you're both on the same page.

4) *Evaluate.* Give it a month or two and then evaluate. How are the kids doing together? Is the day/time working well? Anything need to be adjusted?

5) *Enjoy.* Your family will likely sense a difference in you when you are taking some time for yourself regularly.

Tip: Send meals or snacks with trades. My friend Laura offers this wisdom from experience: "I've found that it can be a big help to the other mom if I send lunches packed and/or snacks along with my kids. It helps to ease mealtime stress and could even be a financial help to not have extra hungry kids to feed. A dear friend and I have traded kids a lot over the years and we almost always offer this to each other. When she's kept my kids overnight, I've sent along a freezer meal for her to either use while my kids are there, or save for later. This helps me feel like I'm not 'asking too much' of her, and also helps her out in a practical way."

BETTER TOGETHER BABYSITTING CO-OP

Date Night Swaps and Sitting Trades are great ways to set up regular time for yourself or your marriage. Creating a larger, more formally organized co-op allows you to expand your network of sitters while keeping the trades fair. Here's how to get one started:

1) *Propose.* Find a group of moms/families to whom you can propose the idea of a babysitting co-op. It could be your moms group, your neighborhood, a homeschooling support group, or even a moms meet-up group in your community. Think about families that have similar parenting styles, beliefs, and values as your family.

2) *Pick.* Determine how to keep track of hours. Some groups use tickets, other groups use poker chips, and still others use shared spreadsheets on Google Drive. Whatever you use, make sure you have fifteen-minute, thirty-minute, and one-hour "currency" for your co-op. You'll also need to determine the value of babysitting hours. Will families with more than one child "pay" a higher rate than families with one child? Can a co-op family earn extra credits for caring for kids on holidays?

3) *Determine.* Decide what your membership requirements will be. Will you start everyone out with a certain amount of currency? Will you have meetings? Do members need to use the co-op a minimum number of hours a month? Who is the group open to? Can members join at any time or only when you have quarterly socials? Can anyone join, or do they need to be "sponsored" by someone in the co-op? Are there guidelines for how far in advance you need to schedule or how late you can cancel? If a cancellation happens at the last minute, does the family that cancelled still have to "pay" the family who was reserving the time for them?

4) *Document.* Put everything in writing for co-op members to sign. While this may not be legally binding without lawyer involvement, it will create policy and spell out expectations for everyone. Make sure you cover policies about:

- Ownership and storage of firearms
- Cigarettes
- Medications (how medications are stored in the house and if medication can be given)
- Emergencies: Can the babysitter take your child to the hospital in an emergency?
- Pets

5) *Register.* Create a registration form that provides information about each child and offers full disclosure about the environment of each member's home. In addition to name, address, email, and cellphone info, make sure to include whether there are pets, firearms, or cigarettes in the home. Also make sure each child's age, birth date, and allergies are

notated. This information could be shared on an accessible Google doc so parents can make informed decisions about their child's care.

6) *Socialize.* Most families are far more comfortable leaving their children with people they know. You might want to plan monthly or quarterly social settings where families can get to know one another. A regular playgroup or "meet at the park" get-together can also be a great way to become familiar with another. Don't hesitate to do a moms night out or dads night out gathering so you can occasionally have adult conversation with other parents in your group!

33 BIBLE VERSES TO SHARE
WITH A FRIEND GOING THROUGH A HARD TIME

James 1:2–4 Count it all joy, my brothers, when you meet trials of various kinds, for you know that the testing of your faith produces steadfastness. And let steadfastness have its full effect, that you may be perfect and complete, lacking in nothing.

Romans 5:3–5 But we also glory in our sufferings, because we know that suffering produces perseverance; perseverance, character; and character, hope. And hope does not put us to shame, because God's love has been poured out into our hearts through the Holy Spirit, who has been given to us.

Proverbs 18:10 The name of the LORD is a strong tower; the righteous man run into it and is safe.

Exodus 15:2a The LORD is my strength and my song; he has given me victory.

Psalm 9:9–10 The LORD is a refuge for the oppressed, a stronghold in times of trouble.

Isaiah 26:4 Trust in the LORD forever, for the LORD GOD is an everlasting rock.

1 Chronicles 16:11 Seek the LORD and his strength; seek his presence continually!

Psalm 32:7–8 You are my hiding place; you will protect me from trouble and surround me with songs of deliverance.

1 Peter 5:7 Cast all your anxiety on him because he cares for you.

Isaiah 12:2 Behold, God is my salvation; I will trust, and will not be afraid. For the LORD GOD is my strength and my song, and he has become my salvation.

2 Timothy 1:7 For God did not give us a spirit of timidity, but a spirit of power, of love and of self-discipline.

Exodus 33:14 My presence will go with you, and I will give you rest.

Deuteronomy 31:8 It is the LORD who goes before you. He will be with you; he will not leave you or forsake you. Do not fear or be dismayed.

Deuteronomy 33:27 The eternal God is your refuge, and underneath are the everlasting arms.

Psalm 34:17 When the righteous cry for help, the LORD hears and delivers them out of all their troubles.

Isaiah 43:1–3 Fear not, for I have redeemed you; I have called you by name, you are mine. When you pass through the waters, I will be with you; and through the rivers, they shall not overwhelm you; when you walk through fire you shall not be burned, and the flame shall not consume you. For I am the LORD your God, the Holy One of Israel, your Savior.

John 14:27 Peace I leave with you; my peace I give you. I do not give to you as the world gives. Do not let your hearts be troubled and do not be afraid.

Psalm 34:4 I sought the LORD, and he answered me and delivered me from all my fears.

Philippians 4:13 I can do everything through him who gives me strength.

2 Thessalonians 3:3 But the Lord is faithful, and he will strengthen you and protect you from the evil one.

Isaiah 40:29 He gives power to the weak and strength to the powerless.

Psalm 27:1–3 The LORD is my light and my salvation—whom shall I fear? The LORD is the stronghold of my life—of whom shall I be afraid? When the wicked advance against me to devour me, it is my enemies and my foes who will stumble and fall. Though an army besiege me, my heart will not fear; though war break out against me, even then I will be confident.

Joshua 1:9 Be strong and courageous; do not be frightened or dismayed, for the Lord your God is with you wherever you go.

Psalm 145:18–19 The LORD is near to all who call on him, to all who call on him in truth. He fulfills the desires of those who fear him; he hears their cry and saves them.

Psalm 138:3 When I called, you answered me; you made me bold and stouthearted.

Psalm 16:8 I have set the LORD always before me; because he is at my right hand, I shall not be shaken.

Psalm 62:1–2 My soul finds rest in God alone; my salvation comes from him. He alone is my rock and my salvation; he is my fortress, I will never be shaken.

Psalm 91:1–2 You who live in the shelter of the Most High, who abide in the shadow of the Almighty, will say to the Lord, "My refuge and my fortress; my God in whom I trust."

2 Corinthians 12:9 My grace is sufficient for you, for my power is made perfect in weakness.

1 Peter 5:10 And the God of all grace, who called you to his eternal glory in Christ, after you have suffered a little while, will himself restore you and make you strong, firm and steadfast.

2 Thessalonians 3:16 Now may the Lord of peace himself give you peace at all times and in every way.

Hebrews 4:16 For we do not have a high priest who is unable to sympathize with our weaknesses, but we have one who in every respect has been tested as we are, yet without sin. Let us therefore approach the throne of grace with boldness, so that we may receive mercy and find grace to help in time of need.

Deuteronomy 31:6, 8 Be strong and bold; have no fear or dread of them, because it is the Lord your God who goes before you. He will be with you; he will not fail you or forsake you. Do not fear or be dismayed.

If you type in these verses at www.BibleGateway.com, you can look them up in different translation versions. This can bring a freshness to a verse you're already familiar with or it can help you understand a verse better if you're new to the Bible. You might specifically look at the New International Version (NIV), English Standard Version (ESV), New Living Translation (NLT), and The Message.

⸺⸺

DEAR LEADER,

*H*earts at Home (www.HeartsatHome.org) is an organization built upon the premise that mothers mother better when they're not alone. Because of that, most of our printed resources are designed to be used either individually or as a group study. If you choose to read this book along with other moms, we believe *Better Together* is a great text for launching life-changing discussions.

The group sessions are organized around the ten chapters, so you should try to plan for ten group meetings. Encourage each mom to have a copy of the book so that she can highlight or mark her copy as she reads— and bring her marked-up copy to your group meetings. You might set right up front, however, that this will be a "no guilt" study. If a mom doesn't have time to read the chapter, make sure she knows she can still come.

The leader's job is to facilitate discussion, and the best group leaders prefer hearing others talk more than listening to themselves. You can't be a perfect leader, but we hope you'll try to be as authentic as possible. Although you may lead by example in answering the questions yourself, you should try to drive the discussion and life-application deeper.

In your preparation time, familiarize yourself with the questions and jot down any additional questions you might present to the group. Pray for group members and for God's guidance.

The Connect questions are designed to be ice-breakers. Use these questions, or a similar question of your own, to open up conversation and get the group talking and sharing.

In your Dig Deep time, do your best to draw out the quieter group members and to move the discussion along if one person tends to monopolize the conversation. If the group gets off the subject, pull the focus back to the question posed.

The Apply section encourages personal reflection and goal-setting. It would be great for group members to go home with one piece of wisdom they want to assimilate into their friendships that week—and some ideas for actions they might take to make the teaching real in their lives.

Be sure to make time for prayer, either having one person close in prayer or sharing a group prayer time. If your group is not really comfortable with praying together, you as the leader may have to take that responsibility of closing in prayer. When you discuss the "Praying Together" chapter, that might be a great time to begin praying together as a group!

Our hope is that this discussion will deepen your group's relationships and broaden each group member's vision of doing life together!

CHAPTER 1: WHERE IT ALL BEGINS

Connect

Have everyone share with the group a little about themselves.

Dig Deep

1) The author states that "friendships change as motherhood changes." What have been your experiences with friendships changing? Has that reality been hard for you to accept?

2) Have you ever been in an environment where you really felt like you belonged? Can you identify what relational elements made that happen?

3) Of the ten benefits of friendship the author lists in chapter 1, which one are you most yearning for right now? Why?

4) Have someone in the group read Hebrews 4:14–16. Have you ever thought about the fact that Jesus understands the challenges of relationships?

Apply

1) Talk to God this week about your friendships. Remember His friends both enriched His life and let Him down. He understands.

2) Connect intentionally with one friend this week. Send her a text, invite her over, meet her for coffee, or give her a call.

Pray

Lord, thank You for bringing us together. Thank You for giving us this opportunity to explore just how we really are better together as moms. Open each of our hearts up to what You want us to learn and where You want us to grow. More than anything, Lord, help us to come to understand how we are really better when we do life together with You. In Jesus' name. Amen.

CHAPTER 2 WHO ARE YOU "MOMMING" WITH?

Connect

Word Association: When you think of friendship, what word comes to mind? Why?

Dig Deep

1) The author states that "true friendships aren't slice and bake; they're made from scratch. They can't be rushed and are the result of time, vulnerability, and commitment." Of those three ingredients—time, vulnerability, and commitment—which one do you struggle with the most? Why?

2) Does striking up a conversation strike fear in your soul? Do you have any strategies you can share that you've found helpful in meeting new people?

3) Are you more of a "Here I Am" person, or are you more of a "There You Are!" person? How can you more intentionally leave your circle broken so groups you are in become "there you are!" groups?

4) Have you ever felt "unfriendable"? How has past rejection colored your current approach to friendships?

5) The author's daughter shares about staying in her moms group for three years before she found an incredible group of friends. How does perseverance figure into friendships?

6) Of the barriers to friendship that the author mentions in chapter 2, which ones do you think you struggle with the most?

Apply

1) Read Proverbs 13:20; Proverbs 22:24–25; and 1 Corinthians 15:33. What principles do these verses offer for forging friendships?

2) Challenge yourself to be a "there you are" person in a school, work, or church environment this week.

3) Write a friend a note this week to let her know how much you appreciate her investment in your life.

Pray

Lord, help us to each evaluate what we contribute both positively and negatively to our relationships. Help us to find the courage to be "there you are" women. Show us how to keep our circles broken—working hard to include and not exclude. Help us to follow Your example to really see people and make them feel valued. In Jesus' name . . . Amen.

CHAPTER 3 VARIETY IS THE SPICE OF LIFE!

Connect

What was your friendship experience as a child? As a teenager?

Dig Deep

1) When you took the Mothering Personality Inventory, what did you discover about yourself? Take each trait one at a time and ask the group members to share which personality trait they are and where they are on

the spectrum. (Note to leader: This will likely be the bulk of this week's Dig Deep discussion.)

2) What do you think about the statement that for many things there's not "right or wrong" but simply "different"? Do you struggle letting your husband, kids, or friends do things differently than you do?

3) In what environments do you most often find yourself comparing yourself to other moms and feeling like you don't measure up?

Apply

1) Text or call a friend to get together this week. If you don't get a response or she's not willing to get together, try someone else. If you're looking to increase your friendship circle, make this a MBF or TBF relationship.

2) Think about how your current friends fit into the Friendship Framework the author talks about. Then think through your friendship expectations and whether they are realistic or not.

Pray

Lord, thank You for the unique way You've created each one of us. Help us to celebrate each other. Help us to embrace the differences and resist the urge to judge one another. May we truly believe that we are each "fearfully and wonderfully made." As we learn more about doing life together, help us to keep our expectations of one another realistic. May we be women of grace and love, and a light to the world around us. In Jesus' name ... Amen.

CHAPTER 4 LEARNING TOGETHER:
"WHAT A GREAT IDEA! I CAN'T WAIT TO TRY THAT OUT!"

Connect

Take a couple minutes and share with the group about the family in which you grew up.

Dig Deep

1) What is one thing you highlighted, underlined, or have been thinking about since reading this chapter? Why did that stand out to you?

2) We gain so much by doing life side by side. Is there something you now do because of a friend's influence on your life?

3) Of all the co-ops mentioned in this chapter, which one most interested you? Are you ready to jump in and make that happen? Why or why not?

Apply

1) What are you doing alone that you could be doing with a friend? Reach out to a friend to suggest a project trade this week.

2) Is there something you are doing that you could learn how to do better from another mom? A project you'd like to accomplish? A daily task? What could you "crowdsource" through social media, in your moms group, or with a group of friends to open up the possibilities?

Pray

Lord, you have given us all different strengths and talents. When we link arms with one another, the possibilities are endless. Instead of feeling less than, help me to see the strengths of the women around me as something positive and helpful to me. Give me the courage to reach out to those around me and find ways to make the tasks of mothering a group effort. May I pursue community like never before. In Jesus' name . . . Amen.

CHAPTER 5 HELPING TOGETHER:
"YOU DON'T HAVE TO DO THAT ALONE. I'LL HELP YOU!"

Connect

What is one household chore you hate doing? Why?

Dig Deep

1) Can you share a time when a friend helped you or you helped a friend? How did that experience affect your friendship?

2) Have you ever done any type of co-op? What was the experience like for you?

3) Have you ever helped organize any neighborhood get-togethers? Ever been a part of a block party or other social that brings together the people who live nearby? What was your experience?

4) What fears have kept you from offering or accepting help?

5) What was the biggest takeaway you had in this chapter?

Apply (choose one or all)

1) Do you have a friend who's trying to get a project done? Offer to help her in some way this week, if your availability allows.

2) Do you have a project you're trying to get finished? Ask a friend to help you!

3) Did any of the co-ops discussed in this chapter interest you? Take a step this week to explore starting a co-op you (and your friends) need!

Pray

Lord, thank You for modeling for us what it looks like to live in community. We know we're better together when we're helping one another. Help us to stop making excuses and start making offers. Help us to resist the fears that keep us from asking for help. Help us to see the needs around us. In Jesus' name . . . Amen.

CHAPTER 6 CARING TOGETHER:
"YOU'RE NOT ALONE. WE'RE HERE FOR YOU."

Connect

Can you share a time in your adult life when you felt genuinely cared for?

Dig Deep

1) Of the eight gifts the author mentions in chapter 6, can you share a time when you were on the receiving end of one of those gifts?

2) Brainstorm some practical ways to care for a new mom, a tired mom, or a mom in crisis.

3) Have you ever considered yourself being in the "ministry of availability"? How do you live that out as a friend?

Apply

Who needs to know you care? Choose one of the eight gifts in chapter 6 to give a friend this week.

Pray

Lord, You genuinely cared for others. You saw their need and met it. Help us to do the same in our circle of friends. May we be women of compassion and kindness, sharing Your hope with those around us. In Jesus' name . . . Amen.

CHAPTER 7 SHARING TOGETHER:

"REALLY? YOU FEEL THAT WAY TOO?"

Connect

What's your faith story?

Dig Deep

1) What "experience stories" do you have that could possibly help someone else?

2) In what ways have your stories limited you? Are there any of your stories that have launched you?

3) Share one of your experience stories with the group. How was God a part of that story? How can you share that story so it's more about what God did than what you did?

Apply (choose one or all)

1) Think through and jot down your experience stories. This is a first step to sharing your stories.

2) If your story is leaking out in ways that are not relationally helpful, take the next step into healing and hope. Contact a friend, a pastor, or a counselor to help you unpack your story.

3) Ask God to show you someone who needs to hear your experience story. Then be brave and share it to give her hope and help.

Pray

Lord, thank You for this study. It's stretching and strengthening us. Help us to see our stories as a way to talk about what You've done in our lives. Help us to see opportunities to share our stories. More than anything, help us to be defined by You and You only. In Jesus' name . . . Amen.

CHAPTER 8 PRAYING TOGETHER:

"I'M STANDING IN THE GAP FOR YOU."

Connect

How was prayer a part of your growing-up years?

Dig Deep

1) What has been one strategy you've found helpful for reading the Bible?

2) Does the thought of praying aloud in a group intimidate you or invigorate you? Why?

3) What part of friendship or prayer is awkward to you? What "awkward" do you need to push through to get to a new normal?

Apply

1) Do you have a friend going through a tough time? Send her a prayer text today!

2) Are you going through a tough time? Ask a friend to partner in prayer with you.

Pray

Lord, we confess that we too often try to go it alone. We don't even think to talk to You. We forget the power of Your Word. Help us to draw our strength from You each day. Prompt us to pray. May we never forget that we are better when we do life together with You! In Jesus' name . . . Amen.

**CHAPTER 9 FORGIVING TOGETHER:
"I'M SORRY, I LET YOU DOWN."**

Connect

If you did a two-day getaway with a friend, what would you do?

Dig Deep

1) Have you ever experienced a friendship breakup? What did you learn in that experience?

2) Read Matthew 18:15. How do we practically carry that out?

3) Have you ever experienced a toxic friendship? If so, how did you decide to handle it? What did you learn through the experience?

Apply

1) Evaluate your friendships. Are there any that are naturally fading? Is that okay with you or do you need to make some intentional investments?

2) Do you have any friendship fiascos you need to tend to?

3) How are you doing with forgiveness and grace?

4) Of the four "Be Attitudes" in this chapter, which one do you need to focus on the most?

Pray

Lord, we confess that we've been hurt by someone we've called a friend. That hurt causes us to put up walls as a form of protection. We know those walls keep us disconnected from others. Help us to forgive. Help us to move forward. Help us to be women of love and grace. In Jesus' name . . . Amen.

CHAPTER 10 ENCOURAGING TOGETHER: "YOU'VE GOT THIS! YOU CAN DO IT!"

Connect

If you could take a one-week vacation to anywhere in the world, where would you go? Why?

Dig Deep

1) When has another mom's honesty helped you feel normal?

2) "Letting another mom peek into your imperfect life can sometimes be the best encouragement you can offer." What's undone at your house right now that you could share with the group so someone else will know she's not alone?

3) Have you ever received encouragement from a stranger? Have you ever given encouragement to a stranger? How did either of those situations make you feel?

4) Talk about what encourages you the most. Brainstorm practical ways to encourage a friend.

Apply

Print out the Better Together commitment found on www.bettertogeth-erbook.org. Hang it somewhere where you'll see it on a regular basis to remember the principles of this study.

Pray

Lord, You didn't do life alone on this earth. You modeled community and showed us what it looks like to do life with others. Help us to be cheerleaders for one another. When we're tempted to be critical, convict us of our judgment and shut our mouth. Help us to understand the power of our positive words in friendship. In Jesus' name. Amen.

ACKNOWLEDGMENTS

This book is a project of collaboration in the truest sense. Not only have we shared our stories, but many of our friends have allowed us to share theirs as well. Specifically we want to express our appreciation to:

Every mom who has shared her story, frustrations, joys, and discoveries with us. Each story has helped formulate the message of this book.

The beautiful people who make up the Hearts at Home leadership team. It is a joy to serve with such a wonderful group of men and women.

Our pre-readers who gave valuable initial feedback: Megan, Karla, Beth, Rachel, Laura, Angie, Brenda, Bonnie, Erin, Becky, Christina, Leah, and Lori. You guys rock! Thank you for reading, challenging, adding thoughts, asking questions, creating sticky statements, and making suggestions. You have all made this a better book!

Our prayer team: Thank you for standing in the gap for us!

The Moody Publishers team: We love partnering with all of you on our Hearts at Home books!

Our families: Thank you for cheering us on and believing in us.

God: Thank You for Your grace and love. Life is truly better doing it together with You!

*ear Reader,*

*We'd love to hear how this book has encouraged you personally!
Let's connect online!*

Jill Savage

Email: jillsavagespeaking@heartsathome.org
Website/Blog: www.JillSavage.org
Facebook: www.facebook.com/jillsavage.author
Twitter: @jillsavage
Instagram: @jillsavage.author

Anne McClane

Email: amcclane@heartsathome.org
Website/Blog: www.everydaylittlethings.com
Facebook: www.facebook.com/anne.mcclane
Twitter: @annemcclane
Instagram: @annemcclane

Hearts at Home

Email: hearts@heartsathome.org
Website/Blog: www.HeartsatHome.org
Facebook: www.facebook.com/heartsathome
Twitter: @hearts_at_home
Instagram: @heartsathome

Make sure you check out www.bettertogetherbook.org, where you'll
find additional resources to encourage you and to equip you to lead a
book study, if you desire.

Joining you in the journey,
Jill and Anne

HEARTS
at HOME

The Go-To Place for Moms

*H*earts at Home's mission is to encourage, educate, and equip every mom in every season of motherhood, using Christian values to strengthen families. Founded in 1993, Hearts at Home offers a variety of resources and events to assist women in their roles as wives and mothers.

Hearts at Home is designed to provide you with ongoing education and encouragement in your journey of motherhood. In addition to this book, our resources include the Heartbeat Radio Program and our extensive Hearts at Home website, blog, and eCommunity. We also offer a monthly free eNewsletter called *Hearts On-The-Go* as well as daily encouragement on Facebook and Twitter.

Additionally, Hearts at Home conference events make a great getaway for individuals, moms groups, or for enjoying time with that special friend, sister, or sister-in-law. The regional conferences, attended by more than ten thousand women each year, provide a unique, affordable, and highly encouraging weekend getaway for any mom in any season of motherhood.

Hearts at Home
1509 N. Clinton Blvd.
Bloomington, IL 61701
Phone: (309) 828-MOMS
Email: hearts@heartsathome.org